T0079719

BISCUITS AND COOKIES

Edible

Series Editor: Andrew F. Smith

EDIBLE is a revolutionary series of books dedicated to food and drink that explores the rich history of cuisine. Each book reveals the global history and culture of one type of food or beverage.

Already published

Apple Erika Janik · *Banana* Lorna Piatti-Farnell
Barbecue Jonathan Deutsch and Megan J. Elias · *Beef* Lorna Piatti-Farnell
Beer Gavin D. Smith · *Berries* Heather Arndt Anderson
Biscuits and Cookies Anastasia Edwards · *Brandy* Becky Sue Epstein
Bread William Rubel · *Cabbage* Meg Muckenhoupt · *Cake* Nicola Humble
Caviar Nichola Fletcher · *Champagne* Becky Sue Epstein
Cheese Andrew Dalby · *Chillies* Heather Arndt Anderson
Chocolate Sarah Moss and Alexander Badenoch
Cocktails Joseph M. Carlin · *Coffee* Jonathan Morris
Corn Michael Owen Jones · *Curry* Colleen Taylor Sen
Dates Nawal Nasrallah · *Doughnut* Heather Delancey Hunwick
Dumplings Barbara Gallani · *Edible Flowers* Constance L. Kirker
and Mary Newman · *Eggs* Diane Toops · *Fats* Michelle Phillipov
Figs David C. Sutton · *Game* Paula Young Lee
Gin Lesley Jacobs Solmonson · *Hamburger* Andrew F. Smith
Herbs Gary Allen · *Herring* Kathy Hunt · *Honey* Lucy M. Long
Hot Dog Bruce Kraig · *Ice Cream* Laura B. Weiss · *Lamb* Brian Yarvin
Lemon Toby Sonneman · *Lobster* Elisabeth Townsend
Melon Sylvia Lovegren · *Milk* Hannah Velten · *Moonshine* Kevin R. Kosar
Mushroom Cynthia D. Bertelsen · *Nuts* Ken Albala · *Offal* Nina Edwards
Olive Fabrizia Lanza · *Onions and Garlic* Martha Jay
Oranges Clarissa Hyman · *Oyster* Carolyn Tillie · *Pancake* Ken Albala
Pasta and Noodles Kantha Shelke · *Pickles* Jan Davison · *Pie* Janet Clarkson
Pineapple Kaori O'Connor · *Pizza* Carol Helstosky
Pomegranate Damien Stone · *Pork* Katharine M. Rogers
Potato Andrew F. Smith · *Pudding* Jeri Quinzio · *Rice* Renee Marton
Rum Richard Foss · *Salad* Judith Weinraub · *Salmon* Nicolaas Mink
Sandwich Bee Wilson · *Sauces* Maryann Tebben · *Sausage* Gary Allen
Seaweed Kaori O'Connor · *Shrimp* Yvette Florio Lane
Soup Janet Clarkson · *Spices* Fred Czarra · *Sugar* Andrew F. Smith
Sweets and Candy Laura Mason · *Tea* Helen Saberi · *Tequila* Ian Williams
Tomato Clarissa Hyman · *Truffle* Zachary Nowak · *Vodka* Patricia Herlihy
Water Ian MilleR · *Whiskey* Kevin R. Kosar · *Wine* Marc Millon

Biscuits and Cookies

A Global History

Anastasia Edwards

REAKTION BOOKS

For Sacha and Iona

Published by Reaktion Books Ltd
Unit 32, Waterside
44–48 Wharf Road
London N1 7UX, UK
www.reaktionbooks.co.uk

First published 2019
Copyright © Anastasia Edwards 2019

Printed and bound in China by 1010 Printing International Ltd

A catalogue record for this book is available from the British Library

ISBN 978 1 78914 049 1

Contents

Introduction

'Oh damn it, can't a man have a biscuit?!'
Lord Chandos, when asked during the Second World War
to give up one of his pastry cooks

From New York City's Grand Central Station to the remotest
Himalayan outpost, one can always find a biscuit, or its American
sibling the cookie. Whether it is an intensely sweet, soft
chocolate chip cookie bought from a chain store such as Mrs
Field's, or a dusty packet of rich tea biscuits at a climbers' base
camp in Nepal, this humble foodstuff has found a permanent
place in the global modern diet. Eaten at breakfast, lunch and
dinner, and at every point in between, biscuits can be a meal
in themselves or a snack, or neither: a small, often perfectly
formed food eaten, like many contemporary 'interval foods',
almost unconsciously.

One of the few foods that one would never eat with cut-
lery, let alone take a knife to, there is something personal, even
intimate, about biscuits and cookies. In many countries, biscuits, in the form of rusks, are a baby's first food, a tactile
transition from the mother's breast, the perfect introduction
to self-feeding. Biscuits can also be extremely formal: they
feature at royal teas and state banquets. Some shops, such

A wealthy British family being served tea and biscuits, unknown artist,
c. 1745.

as Ladurée, which sells multicoloured and multi-flavoured
macarons (French macaroons), have come to rival the most
expensive chocolatiers in their presentations (and prices).

There are biscuits for every budget and occasion, and
biscuits have even crossed over into the animal world: the
global dog biscuit industry is worth hundreds of millions of
dollars, and one can even buy kits to home-bake special biscuits for deserving pets. The Communion wafer, a descendant
of one of the world's oldest biscuits, has for centuries been
consumed by millions of Christians every Sunday and at key
dates in the Christian calendar.

In many cultures the ubiquity of biscuits has seeped
into the vernacular and features in many expressions. In New
Zealand, travelling 'biscuit class', a play on business class,
implies travelling on provincial flights during which tea and
a biscuit, as opposed to a full meal, is served. In Canada, to

'have had the biscuit' means to 'no longer be good for anything'. In England, when something 'takes the biscuit', it means it is remarkable in some funny or negative manner, as when P. G. Wodehouse wrote in a letter of March 1925, 'Of all the poisonous, foul, ghastly places, Cannes takes the biscuit with absurd ease.' And, contrary to the image of the

A wealthy Venetian woman, accompanied by her family chaplain and possibly her husband, receives an escort who toys with her dog. The ring-biscuit may well carry erotic overtones. Painting by Pietro Longhi (Pietro Falca), 1746.

A French copper Communion wafer box, or pyx, made in Limoges in 1250 using the champlevé enamelling technique.

cookie as a panacea, in America, to 'toss one's cookies' means to vomit, which, in some instances, is just 'the way the cookie crumbles' – in other words, a matter of fate. A 'cookie' has become a common term in Internet commerce and is one that most people around the world will frequently come across, even if they do not otherwise speak English.

Many biscuit and cookie names, such as 'Greek bread', offer fascinating etymological tales. A large, oblong, lightly yeasted sugar biscuit scented with cinnamon and topped with demerara sugar, Greek bread has been popular in Brussels for more than two hundred years. The name comes from a Brussels street called Wolvengracht, from where a community of Augustinian monks traditionally passed out bread to the poor. The bread became known as *de Gracht*, which in Belgian is pronounced 'grecht', which in turn sounds like the French word for 'Greek'. Over the years the bread became refined into biscuits, although they were still referred to as 'bread', and when the French occupied Belgium they translated the name to *pain à la grècque*, or 'Greek bread'.

Such specifically documented metamorphoses are rare, and in many cases food scholars can only theorize as to a biscuit's etymological origins, as for example with *gydingakökur*. A firm fixture of the Icelandic Christmas sugar cookie repertoire, *gydingakökur* translates roughly as 'Jewish cakes'.

Biscuits called 'Greek bread' have been a speciality of the Belgian city of Brussels since the early 1800s.

Iceland's baking heritage crossed the seas from Denmark, which historically had a small Jewish community, and one assumes that this is where the name comes from.

The biscuit's global omnipresence is a recent phenomenon. For much of their history sweet biscuits and cookies were the bridesmaids rather than the bride: they possessed neither the festive standing of the cake (a later invention) nor the nutritional centrality and spiritual significance of bread, although they are related to both these foodstuffs. It was only in the late nineteenth century that biscuits became globally ubiquitous. Prior to this, sweet biscuits, dependent on costly sugar – once called 'white gold' because of the prices it commanded – would have been a rare treat for all but the wealthiest. Furthermore, ovens, essential to most forms of biscuit- and cookie-making, were a rarity in most homes until the nineteenth century.

Biscotti, made using the twice-baked method, are one of the oldest forms of biscuit.

Ship's biscuit, England, 1875. The world's oldest extant fragment of a ship's biscuit dates from 1784.

Unsweetened biscuits, on the other hand, have played a central, if unsung, role in global civilization. Until about 150 years ago, most people, when thinking of biscuits, would have pictured something largely unfamiliar to us today: ship's biscuit, or hardtack. Ship's biscuit was a simple mixture of flour and water baked to such dryness that it could be kept for months, if not years – a fragment from 1784 remains in the collections of the Royal Maritime Museum in Greenwich, London. It was the staple that kept sailors alive at sea when all other provisions had been consumed or had rotted; on land, it has been richly documented as a staple of soldiers since Roman times.

Ship's biscuit was nutrition stripped to its most basic form: unembellished, utilitarian calories offering little satisfaction except, in extreme circumstances, the knowledge that eating them might ensure one's survival. Because of their association with the perils of exploration, war and empire-building, biscuits at one time had a dark side in people's imagination, an aura of drama and potential dearth, even of desperation. In William Shakespeare's *As You Like It*, one character refers to the brain of a dim-witted character as being 'as dry as the remainder biscuit / After a voyage'. Some 120 years later, in 1719, the fictional hero of what many consider to be the first novel in the English language, the eponymous, shipwrecked Robinson Crusoe, recounts, 'Having perceived my bread had been low a great while, now I took a survey of it, and reduced myself to one biscuit-cake a day, which made my heart very heavy.' Crusoe is perhaps the most legendarily self-sufficient character in Western literature, and yet, in his psyche, his survival is powerfully linked to biscuits.

Biscuits also figure poignantly in the accounts of an actual marooned adventurer, Scott of the Antarctic. Prior to his fatal expedition to the South Pole, Captain Scott had worked with the great Victorian biscuit manufacturers Huntley & Palmers to develop special biscuits to take on the voyage. In January 1911, a few months into the expedition, he wrote to the company, saying, 'I have much pleasure in informing you that the various kinds of biscuits supplied by you to this Expedition have given every satisfaction.'[1]

In Scott's story two otherwise discrete streams of the biscuit's history converge: eating biscuits for basic survival, and eating biscuits for pleasure. This book will focus largely on the latter: the mostly sweet and pleasurable biscuits familiar to us today. Some earlier non-sweet biscuits will be mentioned, as they form part of the sweet biscuit's crucial back story, but some important subspecies, such as the cracker and the cheese biscuit, are too important to be mentioned in passing and deserve their own book.

The biscuits and cookies included in this book mostly share the following hallmarks: they are sweet; they are small enough to be eaten with one hand; they are often crisp, except if they are a cookie or a macaroon; they are eaten as a snack or a treat, and not as part of a formal meal; and they are either called biscuits or cookies in their respective countries (or a word that translates into such in English) or else, like the wafer, commonly grouped with biscuits in recipe books or in shops and markets.

Dryness, a paramount characteristic of biscuits according to many, merits a special narrative. In 1991 the British tax authorities decided that all cakes and biscuits, except for chocolate-covered biscuits – deemed 'luxury' items – should be free from value-added tax (VAT). McVitie's, manufacturers of the Jaffa Cake, a chocolate-dipped amalgam of a thin layer of sponge and a layer of orange-flavour jam, thus set out to prove that the Jaffa Cake was a cake, and not a luxury biscuit. They made a huge, cake-sized Jaffa Cake and demonstrated

The Jaffa Cake, a popular British biscuit, was the subject of a tribunal about the true definition of a biscuit.

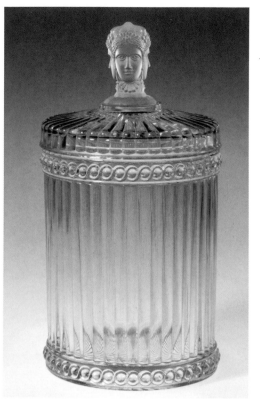

An American biscuit jar designed by John Ernest Miller and manufactured by the Duncan & Miller Glass Company in Pittsburgh, Pennsylvania, between 1878 and 1890.

that because it became hard as it got stale, this proved that it was a cake and not a biscuit, which they argued would go soft. McVitie's won the case, but this changes nothing about the consumption of this 'cake', which remains biscuit-like in every sense: it is too small and fragile to stick a birthday-cake candle into, has a very long shelf life, and is permanently domiciled with the biscuits on the supermarket shelves.

According to *The Oxford Companion to Food*, 'Biscuit varieties, both home baked and factory made, are so numerous that no one has ever catalogued them all, worldwide.'[2] In fact, a list of merely the most popular would fill this book from cover to cover. The book thus focuses on major developments in the biscuit's history through a handful of key biscuits, to which the Appendix, a whistle-stop tour of the global biscuit tin, acts as a companion.

Biscuits have crossed borders, and so certain types of biscuits, such as the wafer and macaroon, feature prominently in the gastronomic histories of several different countries. Rather than cite all their appearances – which might in itself fill a chapter – the examples will often draw for the most part from a single country. If many of the biscuits and cookies described seem to come from Europe and America, it is

Biscuit tins spawned their own art form, starting in the late 19th century, and many have become collector's items, such as this one for Abernethy Biscuits, *c.* 1920s.

'Have wan of your Wife's biscuit!', albumen silver print stereograph, American, 1901.

because sweet biscuits and cookies have largely been made from wheat flour, and hence have evolved from bread cultures rather than, say, the rice cultures of South and East Asia.

Like much of gastronomic and social history, the biscuit's and cookie's histories have operated under the radar of world events. There was no great battle of the biscuit to demarcate the beginning of the early modern period or any great treaty of the cookie to signify its end, but the book nonetheless follows a conventional historical progression.

Finally, an important note to American readers: the word 'biscuit' will be used throughout unless a cookie is what is specifically meant, 'cookie' being a word that only came into American English in the eighteenth century and was not widely used until the twentieth.

I

Survival and Celebration: Fifth Century BC to 1485

He sang quavering like a nightingale; he sent her mead, and wines
sweetened and spiced, and wafers piping hot from the coals.
Geoffrey Chaucer, 'The Miller's Tale'

Neolithic peoples technically had the ability to make biscuits
– having the grain, flour, water and heat – but they had other
priorities. While remains of baking have been found at Neolithic sites in Europe, these could just as easily have been the
remains of proto-bread or a proto-pancake, or indeed a form
of baked porridge. In ancient Egypt, similarly, remains of
what archaeologists have variously called 'biscuit' or 'cake'
have been found in tombs, but we know too little to be certain
of whether or not these are true ancestors of the biscuit. In
ancient Greece and Rome savoury biscuits developed as an
important and discrete foodstuff, laying a technical foundation
for the sweeter biscuits and cookies that would come later.

Ancient Survival

Paximadia, still a staple in Greece today, were made by baking
a loaf of bread made from barley flour, cutting the loaf into

Paximadia have been consumed continuously since ancient Greek times.

slices, and baking those slices a second time until they dried out, resulting in a crisp rusk that could keep for several months. This method came to be known as *panis biscotis*, or 'twice-cooked bread', and provides the root of the English-language word 'biscuit' as well as the root for the French *biscuit*, the Italian *biscotto* and derivations in other languages. This technique of twice-baking survives in popular contemporary biscuits and cookies such as the Italian biscotti, almond biscuits that are often served with sweet wine at the end of a meal, instead of dessert.

The name *paximadia* is thought by some to commemorate a Hellenistic Greek cookery writer called Paxamus, and they were eaten both by sailors and by people on land.[1] Paximadia were a creative use for barley, the staple grain at the time. On board ship, paximadia would have been eaten plain or perhaps soaked with water; on land they were eaten with other foods, for example soaked in soup – a quick and nutritious way by which to consume carbohydrates. They can still be found everywhere in Greece today – they are sold in myriad forms, and competing brands occupy several shelves in supermarkets and bakeries. While some versions are made with only barley, most are made with wheat or a mixture of the two.

The Greeks exerted their intellectual and culinary influence widely, and descendants of the paximadia are still found across Europe. In Puglia, in an area of Italy once known as Magna Graecia, or 'Great Greece', a twice-baked biscuit known as *frisedda* or *frisella* is still eaten, often with chopped tomatoes, thus forming the basis of a convenient, quick and nutritious meal.

Roman Empire

The Roman Empire had its own version of twice-cooked bread, the *bucellatum* – a ring-shaped biscuit, variations of which can still be found across Italy. Similar to the way in which paximadia became associated with sea travel, the bucellatum became associated with movement across land

Cantucci and Vin Santo are a popular dessert in Tuscany and in Italian restaurants abroad.

and came to have strong military associations. The *Secret History*, the sixth-century Greek scholar Procopius' exposé of Emperor Justinian, tells how Justinian and two fellow soldiers travelled on foot to Byzantium, arriving with only biscuits in their cloak pockets.

By the fourth century, the utter necessity and thus ubiquity of the bucellatum in the life of the Roman army was such that soldiers themselves became known as *bucellarii*, and one of the military divisions of the empire was even called Bucellerius, or 'biscuit-eater'.[2] This naming of soldiers after dry biscuits crops up elsewhere in the world's military history, such as during the American Civil War, when soldiers were sometimes referred to as 'hardtacks'.

If we had to pinpoint the first sweet proto-biscuit or proto-cookie, we might glance at Rome to *Apicius*, the name given to a collection of Latin recipes that evolved over the years and was still being printed in the Middle Ages. In the section entitled 'Luxury Dishes', along with the copious recipes for cooking 'sterile wombs' and other forms of offal,

Stereograph showing a Union captain sitting on a crate of hardtack during the American Civil War (1861–5), published *c.* 1880s. American Civil War soldiers were often known as 'hardtacks'.

are eight or nine 'sweet recipes'. One of these instructs the cook to:

> Take coarse wheat flour, cook in hot water in such a way that you make a very thick porridge, then spread it out in a dish. When it has cooled down, cut it up like sweets and fry in best-quality oil. Take them out, pour on honey, sprinkle with pepper, and serve. A better result is obtained if you use milk instead of water.[3]

Although this technique is very different from contemporary baking of sweet biscuits and cookies – it is, in fact, closer to a fritter – the ensuing combined effect of crunch, sweetness and sense of occasion would be familiar to us today. Although the honey is added as a condiment rather than as an ingredient, the recipe presages, in the centuries before the wide availability of sugar, a love of sweetness and an association of sweetness with a certain specialness.

Wafers

If biscuits in the ancient world had a largely utilitarian purpose, in the Middle Ages they began to be eaten as a form of pleasure and celebration. The most significant biscuit of the Middle Ages, and perhaps of all time, was the wafer. Although in its earliest incarnations it was not sweet, it helped generate a tradition of biscuit-eating that survives to this day. The most protean biscuit of all, it is the origin of the ice cream cone and a forefather of the waffles that are served with maple syrup for breakfast in America and of street snacks all over Europe. From the early Middle Ages until the present, the wafer has been consumed at every level of society, in

würden auf Brod geklebt.

This 19th-century German lithograph of crucified Christs was intended to be cut into individual pieces, attached to wafers and swallowed for sickness.

situations ranging from the profane celebrations of a local feast to the sacred ritual of Communion. Its popularity is signalled through its etymology: thought to derive originally from the German verb *weben*, to weave, because of the honey-comb-like design on its face, this became *wafel*, *wafele*, *waffle* and also *wafer* in Middle Dutch. In medieval France, *wafer* became *gwafre* and then *gauffre*.[4]

The wafer has its origins in the unleavened matzo bread that Jews have been eating for millennia at Passover. From this early Jewish custom emerged the medieval European clerical practice of using special irons to prepare the Communion host, especially convenient for missionaries to foreign lands.

In 1270 the guild of Oblayeurs was founded in Paris. Because the French clergy required far more wafers than they could make themselves to distribute to the poor on Maundy Thursday, Oblayeurs – which stems from *oublie*, a corruption of the Latin *oblatum*, meaning 'host' – were permitted to produce them. These lay bakers soon started making non-sacramental wafers and found a way to work round the natural brittleness of wafers by rolling them while still warm and soft. These became known as *oublies*, and the founding of this guild presaged the modern biscuit manufacturing industry.

Many of the wealthiest households in Europe had conferies dedicated to the making of these biscuits, and wafers almost

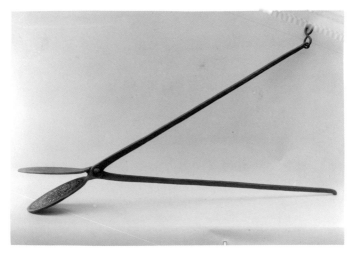

Wafering iron made from cast iron in Umbria, Italy, 1481.

invariably featured at the end of medieval banquets, when they would be drunk with Hippocras, a sweetened wine, in a sort of secular homage to the Eucharist. While it is unclear to what extent these wafers were sweetened (most probably with honey), they were associated with sweetness both through the wines and also in relation to the other confections they were served with. In England wafers are mentioned in the late thirteenth-century *Treatise* of Walter of Bibbesworth, an Anglo-Norman text written to teach young children French and which includes possibly the first full menu of an English feast:

> *Et quant la table fu oustee,*
> *Blaunche poudre oue la grosse dragee,*
> *Maces, quibebes, clougilofrez,*
> *E dautre espiecerye assez,*
> *E oublieie a fuisoun.*

> And when the table was taken away,
> Sweet spice powder with large dragees,
> Maces, cubebs [. . .]
> And enough spicerie,
> And plenty of wafers.[5]

In a book written a century later in Paris, wafers are so indispensable to haut-bourgeois life in the city that they are mentioned several times and feature in what is possibly the first printed shopping list for biscuits, in the form of both savoury and sweet wafers. In *Le Ménagier de Paris* (*c.* 1393; published in English in 1928 as *The Goodman of Paris*), a husband instructs his much younger bride on how to handle a wide variety of domestic situations, including which menus to match to which social occasions. Recalling a wedding feast for forty people, the Goodman recommends that 'From the wafer-maker it behoves to order: first, for the bride's service, a dozen and a half of cheese *gauffres*, 3s.; a dozen and a half of *gros bastons*, 6s.; a dozen and half of *portes*, 18d.; a dozen and a half of *estriers*, 18d.; a hundred sugared *galettes*, 8d.'[6] One can easily picture the hapless, lovelorn Absolon from Chaucer's 'Miller's Tale' approaching one of these vendors to buy 'wafres, piping hoot out of the gleede' (wafers piping hot from the coals) for Alison, the object of his love.

Honey and Spice: German-speaking Europe

Biscuit-making in German-speaking Europe has remained remarkably unchanged over time – in part because of the common language and uniform vocabulary for technical baking terms. It was in the Middle Ages that German biscuits were born, and for centuries they surpassed other biscuits in Europe in their variety of shapes and in the range of spices they contained.

Lebkuchen, a name that encompasses a huge variety of spiced honey biscuits (as well as spiced honey cakes), were the most important and lasting. They were originally made in monasteries, which had generous reserves of honey, the principle sweetener during the Middle Ages and a great preservative. Lebkuchen production gradually also became adopted by specialist guilds, the Lebküchner in Germany and the Lebzelter in Austria. The most famous guild was in Nuremberg, the heart of Bavaria's honey production and a major centre for spice trading.[7] A reference to lebkuchen has been found dating from 1320, although the first recipes date from the sixteenth century.

Modern lebkuchen stall in Achen, Germany.

Bread had been a key component first in pagan central European fertility rites and then in Christian Eucharistic rites, and village bakers in Germany were adept at creating different shaped loaves of bread for different events in the Christian calendar. The development of the biscuit dough, which is much easier to shape precisely than bread dough, allowed bakers to focus more fully on their decorating skills.

Moulds with embossed designs were frequently used to decorate lebkuchen with a rich repertoire of images drawn from folklore and religion. A range of the visual and icono-graphic potential of biscuits is suggested by the collection of one Claus Stalburg, a mayor of Frankfurt in the early six-teenth century, who commissioned forty stone moulds carved by one of the city's top engravers.[8] They include the following sacred and profane subjects: 'How Christ was baptized in the Jordan by John the Baptist', 'Our Lady with Joseph sitting in contemplation surrounded by angels' and 'Three naked women fishing with rods and brining up eel pots'.

Such concrete insights into medieval biscuit history from material culture are rare, and the food historian often must consider more recent biscuit history, using imagination and powers of deduction to effect a handshake with the more remote past. *Leckerli*, from Switzerland, stimulates such a handshake. *Lecker* in High German means 'delicious', and Leckerli are still made in many different forms in Switzerland to mark liturgical holidays. Basel makes the most celebrated leckerli, containing honey and spice, and one bakery is solely dedicated to producing leckerli in a tin shaped like a drum to mark the pre-Lenten Basel carnival, during which pipes and drums are played. Leckerli draw one back to a time when, in the absence of modern distractions and media, the liturgical

Leckerli have been made since medieval times to celebrate liturgical festivals throughout the year. These are a speciality of Basel in Switzerland.

calendar provided the basis of most communal entertainment, and evoke how biscuits might have marked these occasions with celebratory mouthfuls of sweetness and spice.

Commemoration and Celebration

The *Aberffraw* or 'berffro' cake, one of Wales's oldest biscuits, provides a link with the idea of pilgrimages in the Middle Ages. A shortbread-like biscuit with a distinctive scalloped shape, it has been made in the town of Aberffraw, on the island of Anglesey, for centuries. According to locals, one account of the biscuit originates from the moment when, in the early thirteenth century, the wife of the Welsh prince Llewelyn the Great found and admired a scallop shell on the nearby beach. An alternate pedigree points to the fact that Aberffraw biscuits were also called James's cakes, or, in Welsh, *cacennau Iago*. Iago is the Celtic name for James, and the scallop is the symbol of St James. Pilgrims to Santiago de Compostella in Spain traditionally wear scalloped hats. Spain has a strong Celtic tradition, and travel between medieval Wales and Spain is well documented.

Few in the Middle Ages travelled long distances, and fairs provided a popular entertainment to complement liturgical holidays. Cornish fairings carry a long tradition in Britain – and indeed across Europe – of 'fairings', special foods and other objects sold at fairs to be taken home as souvenirs or presents. Biscuits, historically and nowadays, make perfect presents or 'fairings' because of their small size and portability. Many fairs happen at Christmastime, the darkest time of year, and the German *Pomeranzennüsse* and *Pomeranzenbrötchen*, loosely translated as 'orange nuts', hark back to a time when Seville oranges were truly wondrous in the middle of a dark,

Ginger nuts (or ginger snaps), a modern incarnation of a medieval European confection.

cold northern European winter, imparting a refreshing if slightly bitter memory of the sun. They used to be made with the rind of grated or candied Seville oranges, whereas modern versions are made with commercially prepared candy peel.

In Italy, All Souls' Day has for centuries been a popular autumn celebration, and in parts of Italy *fave dei morti* (literally 'beans of the dead'), small biscuits shaped like a broad bean, have long been distributed in order to remind people of their departed loved ones. Historians speculate that the *fave* tradition has roots in ancient Rome, and so one can surmise that it was a feature of medieval European biscuit culture. Also in Italy, in the northeast of the country, godparents have traditionally given *bussolai* to their godchildren on their confirmation day. The ring-shaped bussolai were tied with ribbons and became a visual expression of the celebration.

Bussolai are given to children in northeastern Italy on their confirmation day.

They contain butter, eggs, sugar and *rosolio*, a liqueur that traditionally had tonic properties. They were – and still are – sometimes dipped into wine.

The Middle East

At around the time that the wafer guilds and Lebküchner were being formed in France and Germany, some 4,000 km away in Baghdad, the centre of the Golden Age of Arab civilization, a rich culture of sweet baking had already reached its apogee. It is a legacy that can be seen in any souk in the Middle East or indeed in any Middle Eastern food shop or bakery in the prolific Middle Eastern diaspora: silver platters groaning with baklava, gossamer-thread-like concoctions dripping with honey and cloaked in crushed pistachios.

Middle Eastern baking specializes in pastries and sweetmeats, but biscuits had a firm place in medieval manuscripts. In the *Kitāb al-Tabīkh* (Book of Dishes), written in the thirteenth century by an author most often referred to as Al-Baghdadi, or the Scribe of Baghdad, is the following recipe for *khushkanānaj*, a kind of filled biscuit:

> It is that you take excellent samīd flour and put three ounces of sesame oil on every [pound], and knead it hard, well [with a little water]. Leave it until it ferments, then make it into long cakes, and into the middle of each put its quantity of pounded almonds and sugar kneaded with spiced-rose water. Then gather them as usual, bake them in the brick oven and take them up.[9]

The recipe is notable on several accounts. The mention of 'gather' suggests the possible use of a mould, as in Germany at the same time. 'Khushkanānaj' stems from the Middle Persian, in which *hushk* means 'dry' and *nān* means bread, recalling the relationship between bread and biscuits seen in hardtack. In this recipe the dough is not cooked before being shaped into biscuits, but it might have evolved from an earlier form of hardtack or paximadia.

Like the wafer and lebkuchen, khushkanānaj have survived and proliferated until the present. In one incarnation they are known as *kleicha* and are considered by some to be the 'national cookies' of Iraq. They come in forms such as *kleichat joz*, half-moon-shaped biscuits filled with nuts and sugar, and the moulded *kleichat tamur*, which are filled with dates. One cookbook writer speculates that khushkanānaj have their origins in the *qullupu* biscuits of Mesopotamia and that the name 'kleicha' comes from the term for the dry measure of weight.

Ma'amoul, a Middle Eastern biscuit popular on both Christian and Muslim holidays.

Perhaps the most important legacy of medieval Arabia in terms of biscuit history is an ingredient that the recipes for khushkanānaj and other pastries in the *Kitāb al-Tabīkh* take for granted: sugar. Hardly known in Europe before the twelfth century, it was the Arabs who first introduced sugar to the continent. Its gradual rise in use was to be a silent player in the rise and eventual domination of biscuits and cookies as a global foodstuff.

2
Sweetness and Lightness: 1485–1800

Biskets are generally made in all Seasons, and continue to be part
of the Entertainment throughout the whole year.

François Massialot (1660–1733)

It is impossible to understand the rise of the biscuit in the
early modern period (*c.* 1485–1800) without looking closely at
the history of sugar. In the late Middle Ages sugar was a
luxury even for Europe's royalty, but by the early nineteenth
century it had become a virtual staple throughout European
society. The corollary is clear: as sugar became more available
and cheaper, so biscuits and cookies became more popular.

Eggs are the other defining ingredient of biscuits and
cookies. During the seventeenth century in particular, cooks
came to better understand eggs' ability to impart lightness,
typically when vigorously beaten. This knowledge was dissem-
inated via several popular cookbooks, many of whose authors
were celebrities in their times and who saw themselves as
bridging the gap between the professional expertise of royal
and noble households and a burgeoning middle class. They
were conduits for democratizing once privileged foods, and
biscuits figured in this transition. Wafers continued to be
popular, but biscuits, requiring an oven and new techniques

and ingredients, were an exciting addition to the growing repertoire of dishes served at the tables of the well-to-do. Their sweetness and greater lightness began to create new identities and possibilities, and although the sea biscuit was still very much a feature of maritime and commercial life, sweet biscuits had become, by the end of the eighteenth century, a discrete category of their own, emphasizing pleasure rather than necessity.

Sugar and its Shapes

Introduced to Europe via Venice in the tenth century, sugar, rare and extremely expensive, was initially considered both a spice and a medicine. Throughout the Middle Ages it was used more and more liberally to season savoury dishes, and its use trickled down the social hierarchy. By the sixteenth century sugar was migrating towards a role of its own: a wondrous convergence of science and art that can broadly be called confectionery.

One of the early products of confectionery was the 'soteltie', or 'subtlety'. These 'confections were based primarily on the combination of sugar with oil, crushed nuts and vegetable gums to a make a plastic, claylike substance' that could be sculpted into myriad forms, hardened or baked, and admired for their shape as well as eaten.[1] Early sweet biscuits are an offshoot of confectionery and, in their plasticity of form, can be seen as descendants of the subtlety.

Jumbles are an example of a confection that metamorphosed from sweetmeat to biscuit. The history of the jumble reflects the idea of malleability, a hallmark of biscuit dough, keeping its name but with its ingredients and techniques changing over time and according to different cookery writers

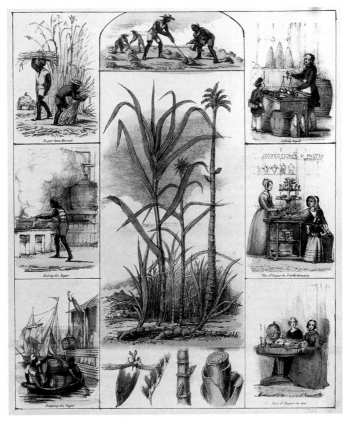

'A sugar cane plant (*Saccharum officinarum*), its flower and sections of stem, bordered by six scenes illustrating its use by man', coloured lithograph, *c*. 1840. The history of the biscuit and cookie is intimately linked to the global history of sugar production.

– recipes for jumbles were still being printed in nineteenth-century cookbooks, though they dwindled in popularity soon after. Some recipes contained eggs and others did not, and some included nuts; while flavourings varied wildly, the hallmark of a jumble was that it could be fashioned into an amusing shape, such as a knot, or into rings or rolls. Jumbles were made in England, France and the Netherlands, where they featured, along with other foods, in several Dutch still-life paintings.

Eggs

In the mid-seventeenth century two seminal cookbooks, both published early in the reign of Louis XIV, indicate that biscuits had fully emerged as a category of their own, separate from the confectionery of the late medieval period. Nicolas de Bonnefons, a valet at Louis' court and the author of books on gardening and cookery, makes no bones about his view that bread is the ultimate food, more important than any other, including meat. A full twenty pages of rich and detailed prose are devoted in his *Les délices de la campagne* (1654) to describing how to bake it. Immediately after the bread recipes come those for wafers and then those for biscuits, a privileged position, coming on the heels of such a passionate overture, and an important signal that biscuits were by then a recognized region in the gastronomic landscape.

As was to be a hallmark of French cooking excellence, Bonnefons' biscuit recipes are written with great precision and polite, if firm, prescription, as the following recipe for an early form of sponge biscuit shows:

Biscuit du Roy

Take a pound of sugar, three quarters of a pound of the finest wheat flour, and eight eggs; beat the lot in a pewter basin with a wooden spatula, until the batter whitens into a foam, and add some lightly crushed fennel seed,

Still-life with Dainties, Rosemary, Wine, Jewels and a Burning Candle, 1607, oil on panel, by celebrated Dutch female painter Clara Peeters.

continue to beat for a good long while after, then dress it in tin *tourtières*, which will need to be buttered lest the dough sticks, after which you dust them with powdered sugar to ice them, and put them in a gentle fire . . . If you want it more delicate, one needs ten eggs, and take out four whites. From the same dough, but a bit firmer, one can make a loaf three inches high, like those thick gingerbreads from Rheims, which after cooling a little, is cut into slices, to serve at table. This was the fashion forty years ago, before the Savoye biscuit was invented, and they called it a pastry cook's loaf [*pain des Pâtissiers*].[2]

If jumbles had roots in medieval confectionery, Bonnefons' *biscuit du roy* anticipated modern baking. The use of eggs in such quantities is key: these are depended upon to raise the

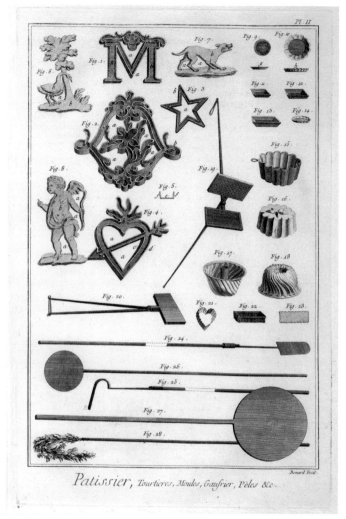

Pl. II

Patissier, *Tourtieres, Moules, Gaufrier, Pèles &c.*

Benard Fecit

Etched plate illustrating the article 'Patissier' in the *Encyclopédie* published by Diderot and D'Alembert, *c.* 1771. Sections and elevations are shown of tin moulds (figs 1–5), almond paste or biscuit cakes in the shape of figures and animals (figs 6–8), tart dishes, a mould and a cake in the form of a Turk's cap (figs 17–18), waffle irons (figs 19–20), a tin dough-cutter in the form of a heart (fig. 21) and utensils for the oven (figs 24–8).

batter and to provide lightness. This lightness takes work. Many cookbooks of the period mandate that the eggs be beaten for at least half an hour to achieve the requisite texture. The foam described by Bonnefons takes at least this much time. The well-to-do households of Europe would likely have had a servant seconded to this task. Today this role can be assumed by modern mixers, though even these take time to metamorphose eggs into foam. Biscuits, for all their smallness and fleeting pleasure, required a commitment of resources.

The recipe also offers other clues to the burgeoning knowledge and accoutrements needed to make biscuits. Bonnefons places emphasis on managing the source of heat, anticipating modern recipes in which preheating and different heat settings for different recipes are used. He also gives alternative methods involving tins or moulds, pointing to the existence of a growing arsenal of baking accessories, evidence of which one can find in any good baking shop today.

With its reference to the 'pastry cook's loaf', Bonnefons' book offers a gift to food historians, and to biscuit historians in particular. For one, his *biscuit du roy* recipe enables us to date roughly the creation of the sponge biscuit. For another, it tells us that in its earliest forms the Savoy biscuit (sponge finger) was still made in the image of a loaf, and so had not quite assumed an identity separate from bread.

Perhaps most importantly, Bonnefons' recipe provides a rare window on to the enterprise of professional biscuit baking. The tension between what experts know and what they are prepared to divulge has always been acute when it comes to baking, which is subject to vagaries such as heat and moisture variations that give even the appliance-rich modern cook cause for grief. Writers such as Bonnefons performed a valuable service in extending their knowledge of techniques to an amateur audience, but they were ostensibly taking business away from professional bakers. The more households baked their own biscuits, the fewer would buy biscuits from bakers. Bakers' guilds were a strong force throughout Europe, and one wonders whether in countries like Germany, the Netherlands and Italy, for instance, these guilds were able to maintain closed ranks. These three countries all produced important cookbooks during this period but, despite having important biscuit cultures, there are hardly any references to biscuits in them.

The influence of Bonnefons' contemporary François Pierre de La Varenne (1615–1678) is felt even more strongly today. Although his name is not attached to it, *Le Pâtissier françois* (The French Pastry Cook), La Varenne's third book, is unique in being the 'only book devoted solely to pastry published in France between the middle of the seventeenth century and the end of the eighteenth'.[3] The author was most vocal about the embargo on baking knowledge imposed by his fellow cooks and raged against the 'ill nature of our most famoustest Pastry Cooks of the French Court, and of the City of *Paris*' to 'smother' knowledge of their art and prevent its dissemination. *Le Pâtissier françois* seeks to 'remedy' this scenario. The book 'doth not contain any composition or mixture which is not very easie to bee prepared, farre more pleasing to the palate, and not at all chargeable to the purse'.[4]

Le Pâtissier françois is a thrilling volume to consult for anyone interested in the foundations of modern baking in all its forms. The chapter on biscuits, containing eight recipes, begins with a detailed master recipe for 'Plain Pastry-chef Biscuits', of which the subsequent seven recipes are basically variations. These include a 'Piedmontese biscuit', showing the extent to which biscuit recipes and techniques crossed borders and developed local variations. The eighth and final recipe is for Lenten biscuits, indicating that biscuits were a

French society ladies eating biscuits, *c.* 1889, by A. Chaillot, in 'Latest Paris Fashions', *Ladies Treasury*, London, March 1889.

common enough part of the diet that they required a suitable substitute for the plentiful 'fast' days of the period.

Occupying a chapter of its own in La Varenne's book is the macaroon. This puffy, soft, pleasurable biscuit has the distinction of being one of the longest-lived biscuits that has undergone the fewest changes to its ingredients and techniques. Despite being a popular fixture throughout Europe and the Middle East, the basic ingredients have remained ground almonds, sugar and egg whites, often flavoured with rosewater. A likely reason for the macaroon's popularity, apart from its deliciousness, was that it could be eaten by Orthodox Jews at Passover – it was technically unleavened, as it was the egg whites that were responsible for raising them. Macaroons crop up throughout the Jewish diaspora in places such as Venice and Budapest. It is also the contemporary biscuit with the most direct ancestry in the early world of confectionery: it progressed from marzipan, which is also made from ground almonds and sugar.

Crunch

One of the qualities that distinguished macaroons was their softness. Increasingly, crispness was a feature valued in sweet biscuits and one that set them apart from larger cakes, bread and confectionery. The cracknell, a biscuit with a long and anomalous history, enshrined this idea in its name. 'Cracknell' is related to the French biscuit *craquelin* and to the Dutch *krakelingen*. In all three languages the sense of the word was of crackling or of crispness.

Despite this consistency of meaning, there was much variation among cracknell recipes, in both ingredients and procedures. The principal difference is that some recipes call for boiling the dough before baking it – a variation on twice-cooking, although in two different mediums – while in others it is baked once, on a sheet, very much like sponge biscuits. One wonders if, like wafers, cracknells were a kind of fair food, consumed on special occasions rather than more frequently.

A feature of many of the boiled cracknells was a curved or hollow form. Both methods were described until at least the eighteenth century. In her famous book *The Compleat Confectioner* (1760), Englishwoman Hannah Glasse still used the boiling method, while a hundred years earlier her countryman Robert May, in *The Accomplisht Cook* (1660), instructed cooks to:

> roule [the dough] very thin, and cut them round by little plats, lay them upon buttered papers, and when they go into the oven, prick them, and wash the tops with the yolk of an egg, beaten and made thin with rose-water or fair water; they will give with keeping, therefore before they are eaten they must be dried in a warm oven to make them crisp.[5]

Crispness was the prominent attribute of what is perhaps the hallmark biscuit of the eighteenth century, the Savoy. This biscuit has survived, under different names, in most European countries – *savoirdi* in Italy, ladyfingers or sponge fingers in the UK. They are consumed in myriad ways: babies suck on them; they are given to children as a light snack; and they are used as a key ingredient in a range of desserts, from the English trifle to the Italian tiramisu.

François Massialot (1660–1733), a successful cookbook writer of the late seventeenth century and chef to members of French royalty, had several recipes for Savoy biscuits. His

The coconut macaroon, one of the many incarnations of a globally popular biscuit.

Krakelingen, a Dutch biscuit celebrated for its crispness.

Rusk biscuits, whose basic recipe dates back to 18th-century Europe, are a popular first snack for babies in many parts of the world.

versions have progressed from Bonnefons' *biscuit du roy*, in that egg whites and yolks are now separated. Working the egg is still tiring, though: 'some Powder-sugar is to be provided of the same Weight as the Eggs, the Whites of which are to be taken, to make the Strongest Snow that possibly can be, by whipping them well with a Whisk.'[6]

Home Baking

The manuscript cookbook of Rebecca Price (1660–1740) shows the popularity of the biscuit from the point of view of a woman managing a household. For Price, baking biscuits did not need the constant mediation of a professional, and her recipes offer a rare insight into the culinary outlook of a woman confident in her abilities and who had mastered making several types of biscuits and enjoyed experimenting.

Price's approach to cooking, especially biscuits, would be familiar to biscuit bakers today. She accumulated recipes from people from many spheres of her life, such as 'my Lady Sheldon', the wife of the Lord Mayor and a prominent London hostess, and cooks at her former boarding school. The following partial list of the biscuit recipes in her manuscript gives a flavour of the junction of influences that was her kitchen:

'Jumbells: my Mothers Receipt'
'Jumbells, or knots, off all cullers, my Aunt Rye's receipt'
'Suger Cakes: My Lady Howe's Receipt'
'Oringe Bisquets: my first Cousen Clerke's Receipt'
'Naple Bisquets: given me at school'

Price is obviously a seasoned baker, and her instructions include caveats such as 'your oven must not be too hott: you must not lay [them] too close one by the other for they will run together' in the case of jumbles, one of nine recipes for these. There is also the sense of a vernacular and shorthand of baking, and an implied understanding that each cook will personalize the biscuit in her own way. In one of her recipes for 'jumbells' she says to 'role them into what fasshon you please', adding that 'if you would have them coullered [coloured], you may take what coullered flowers you please, and take the juce off them, and couller it with that.'[7]

One can almost hear the voices of women – Mrs Burnford, Lady Sheldon – comparing notes and techniques. There is the sense of biscuits as ambassadors for different places. There is a recipe for Naples biscuits – a form of the Savoy biscuit – but also, closer to home, an appreciation of regionalism in such recipes as 'Shrewsbury cakes', named after the town in the West Country of England. This personal yet expansive trend in biscuit baking continues to this day in the 'cookie exchange' parties that take place in the u.s. and in the many forums for exchanging recipes that exist online, some of them largely devoted to biscuits and cookies.

The Birth of the Cookie

Rebecca Price's manuscript is testament to the culinary cross-pollination of her time. One very important foodway – and one of the most important crossroads in biscuit history – was the migration of the Dutch baking repertoire to America, which would eventually lead to the creation of the cookie. In Dutch the word *koek* designates a flat baked item. In seventeenth-century Dutch, *koeckjens* or *koecxkens* were the diminutives of *koek*, and these formed the linguistic root of the American 'cookie'.[8]

The Netherlands has one of the most dynamic baking histories in the world. Pancakes, waffles, wafers, bread, fritters, cakes, pretzels and other biscuits have all been continuously made for centuries in a profusion and variety probably unsurpassed by any country other than Germany. A busy liturgical calendar of feast days has for centuries been marked with specific baked goods, such as *speculaas* (or *speculoos* in Flemish), spiced and buttery biscuits made traditionally on 5 December, St Nicholas's Eve, but biscuits are also eaten non-specifically, year-round, with tea and coffee.

In the seventeenth century, the Dutch Republic was one of the richest states in the world and its people some of the best fed. The still-life paintings of the period reflected the abundance and quality of the table, and many of these included biscuits. A painting of a bakery shop by Job Adriaen-szoon Berckheyde (1630–1693) offers a rare glimpse into biscuit food culture: it is most probably Christmas, and wealthy, fashionably dressed children are in a bakery buying

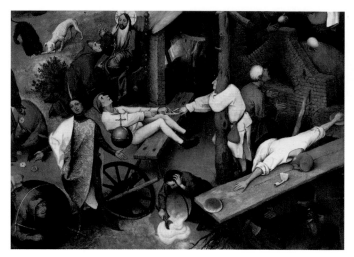

Two men playing a popular game involving pulling a Dutch *krakelingen* biscuit. Detail from the painting *Netherlandish Proverbs* by Pieter Bruegel the Elder, 1559, oil on panel.

sugar biscuits.[9] Little more information exists about this painting, but its simple composition and the calm attitudes of the children suggest that this is an activity that, though special, is not unfamiliar. Biscuit culture, in other words, is part of life, much as buying sweets or candy is a familiar activity to many children in wealthy countries around the world today.

Also in the picture are sweet pretzels, or *krakelingen*, one of those biscuits goods that, like jumbles, cracknells and wafers, have metamorphosed over time and overlapped into other categories, not to mention spawned a trail of 'fakelore' as to their origins. In the early modern period, and indeed until the twentieth century, *krakelingen* were hard and sweet. Indeed in Dutch the word *krakeling* 'is linguistically related both to the verb *kraken*, to crack or crunch, and the noun *krakeel*, meaning quarrel or fight'.[10] In some Dutch Golden Age paintings, such as one by Pieter Bruegel the Elder, *krakelingen* were depicted in a sort of tug-of-war that involved people pulling at the *krakelingen* with their little fingers to see who could come away with the most.[11]

A poem by the book merchant Zacharias Heyns written in 1602, about a very crunchy, buttery biscuit, is further testament to the exuberance surrounding biscuits in the Netherlands:

Kantelings,
They are tall pointy things,
Scabby Heads, so they are known,
But strewn with sugar and cinnamon I own,
You've never eaten anything so good.[12]

Given the manner in which biscuits of various kinds were embedded in seventeenth-century Dutch culture, it is initially surprising that the foremost Dutch cookbook of the time, *Der Verstandige Kock* (The Sensible Cook, 1667), provides recipes for various fritters but none for biscuits. Did the housewives of the Netherlands have their own proto-biscuit exchanges like Rebecca Price in England? Or did the powerful Dutch baking guilds, strong from the Middle Ages to the nineteenth century, closely guard their recipes and techniques?

Early Dutch settlers began arriving in the northeastern part of America, given the name New Netherland, in the early 1600s. Dutch bakers tried to organize a guild in the mid-seventeenth century but were turned down, and no baking guilds were ever formed in the colony. Yet the Dutch brought their tradition of baked goods, including biscuits, with them, and *koeckjens* figure prominently in early settler history.

Some of first mentions of *koeckjens* in New Netherland concerned the trade with Native Americans, who it seems quickly developed a taste for the bread and 'sweet cakes' baked by the settlers. They gladly accepted Dutch baked goods as a fair trade for furs and other items, to such an extent that professional bakers were almost put out of business by amateurs trying to make some money on the side. This became such an issue that the authorities issued several ordinances, such as the following, to try to ban the practice: 'It is found by experience that many, as well of this place as coming from elsewhere, in the trading season make a business to baking Koekjens . . . and short weight white bread for the Indians, to the great loss of the bakers, and quit baking in the winter.'[13] Professional bakers have tried to protect their interests throughout history, but this has to stand as one of the most direct injunctions against amateur participation.

America was largely rural (even in early cities there were few bakeries) and women practised their baking in solitude – a far cry from the densely populated Netherlands, with its sophisticated urban centres. The terms 'biscuits' and 'cookies' were both used to describe the small cakes they baked, but gradually the term 'cookie' gained in popularity, while 'biscuit' came to designate a fluffy, leavened baked good similar to the British scone.

The first American recipes for cookies appear in Amelia Simmons's *American Cookery*. The book was published in 1796 – twenty years after the Declaration of Independence was written – and Simmons claimed that the book was 'adapted to this country and all grades of life'. For those of us familiar with contemporary cookies, the recipe and its results at first seem improbable, an anticlimax:

Cookies

One pound of sugar boiled slowly in half pint of water, scum well and cool, add 1 tea spoon pearlash, dissolved in milk, then two and a half pounds of flour, rub in 4 ounces of butter, and two large spoons of finely powdered coriander seed, wet with above; make rolls half an inch thick and cut to the shape you please; bake fifteen or twenty minutes in a slack oven – good three weeks.

The food journalist and author Andrew Beahrs, who in 2010 decided to make the recipe with his son, started off with high hopes that it would prove to be 'ungodly good' and provide a link with the past. However, the results were unexpected:

Having made it, the original recipe reads differently to me. Simmons could have included eggs, or more butter (she had plenty of both in other recipes). Instead, it seems to me, she wrote with an eye towards hospitality, towards sharing something she thought luxurious. There's plenty of sweetness in our cooking today (too much, in fact)

American 'biscuits', leavened baked goods, are culinarily unrelated to biscuits and cookies.

Sugar cookies are some of the easiest biscuits to bake and decorate at home and can take almost as many forms as there are bakers.

now that sugar, and especially corn syrup, are cheap. But the first cookie recipe – the recipe for a dry, sweet cookie, still very much like a little cake – made me think of a time when sweetness wasn't a cheat, or a mask. It was sugar, and in humble households that was special.[14]

Sugar was to become even cheaper in the nineteenth century and would be supplanted by other forms of sweetness in the twentieth century and beyond. Although biscuits and cookies would eventually be taken for granted, something of their original specialness survives.

3
The Golden Age:
The Nineteenth Century

The biscuit baker, properly so-called, is a being of the past.
Frederick Vine, baker, 1896

The nineteenth century was the golden age of the biscuit. In the early 1800s biscuits and cookies were still a treat, whether made at home or by small bakers, but by the eve of the First World War the sweet biscuit had become the first truly global convenience food, available in most countries of the world and in some consumed on a daily basis. This leap was the result of successive technological 'tipping points', innovations that followed each other in quick succession and which paralleled other advances of the Industrial Revolution. Industrialization turned the biscuit into a commodity, which in turn prompted innovations in packaging and marketing. These set a new standard for many other foods, and the biscuit and the cookie can be seen as early trailblazers for the fast foods that would come to dominate modern life.

Industrialization

The rise of the humble biscuit was so significant that in 1860 a London newspaper, the *Morning Star*, devoted a long article to it:

> Closely allied to our old friend the bread baker . . . is his more modernised relative, the manufacturer of that nutritious, sweet, toothsome little condiment known as a biscuit. Of course we don't mean for a moment to pay a compliment to the great, hulky, ill-conditioned article which serves as one of the bases of England's naval greatness. We have to write about a different genus altogether – of picnics, Osborne's, Queen's, caraways, lunch, coffee and wine biscuits, of cracknels, and nonsuches, and all those little creations which form a part, and a distinguished part, in our social economy, and bear as much relation to the hard-baked compound of flour and water on which sailors feed as does the full-grown intellectual man to the polypus, from which, if modern theorists speak truly, he first derived the power of existence, and launched himself upon the sliding-scale of creation.[1]

In 1860 the Industrial Revolution was in full swing – as was the Social Darwinism to which the article alludes – and in referring to biscuit being part of the 'social economy' of England at the time, the writer clearly points to its indispensability. The biscuit was, in fact, both a product and an enabler of the newly industrialized lifestyle. Technology permitted its increased production, and the newly industrialized workforce demanded foods that required no preparation.

Prior to the Industrial Revolution, breakfasts in England had been larger and served relatively late, at 9 or 10 a.m., and dinner had been served between 4 and 5 p.m. By 1860 the

'Peak Frean Biscuit Manufactory', from the *Illustrated London News*, December 1874, provides detailed insight into the 19th-century mechanization of biscuit production. Such techniques and equipment were exported around the world.

Digestive biscuits are some of the most popular industrially produced biscuits in the UK, especially in their chocolate-coated versions.

Industrial Revolution had so altered the working day that breakfasts had become smaller and were served earlier, typically between 8 and 9 a.m., while dinner had receded to between 7 and 8 p.m. Appetites needed to be sated during this wider gap between meals, and lunch and tea thus became more significant meals – and good opportunities at which to serve biscuits.[2] The new biscuits were functional but they were also pleasurable. The *Morning Star* article makes official the divorce between the sea biscuit and the sweet biscuit: a life of graft was being officially exchanged for a life that promised greater leisure.

As the home of the Industrial Revolution, it is not surprising that England pioneered the large-scale manufacture and export of biscuits and biscuit technology – even the French *Larousse Gastronomique* tips its hat to this accomplishment. One company in particular, Huntley & Palmers, led the charge.

Huntley & Palmers' rise quite neatly follows the trajectory of Queen Victoria's reign (1837–1901). In 1822 a baker named Joseph Huntley opened a small shop in the town of Reading, some 64 km (40 mi.) from London. It was only 5½ metres (18 ft) wide and sat atop a large underground bakehouse. By 1898 Huntley & Palmers had become a limited company, with capital of £2.4 million, producing more than four hundred varieties of biscuit.[3]

Between these dates several technological advances occurred in quick succession. In 1833 Sir Thomas Grant, Superintendent of the Victualling Office at Portsmouth, with the help of engineer Sir John Rennie, invented steam-powered machinery that sped up the mixing, rolling and cutting processes of making ship's biscuits. Before this it had taken 45 men one hour to produce 680 kg (1,500 lb) of biscuits. With the new machinery it took just sixteen men one hour to produce a ton. Quality and uniformity were also improved. Around this time, Jonathan Dodgson Carr, a miller and baker from Carlisle, designed machinery for cutting and stamping biscuits, based on a hand-operated fly-press. Along with simple machinery for kneading, cutting and rolling, this facilitated making 400 tons of biscuits a year.

Garibaldi, known among British schoolchildren as 'squashed fly' biscuits. They were first manufactured in London in 1861 by the biscuit company Peek Frean & Co.

In 1841 George Palmer, trained as a miller and confectioner, introduced a small steam engine to the back of the shop owned by his cousin Thomas Huntley. By 1846, when Palmer moved the business to a factory, the firm's output had doubled, and Palmer adapted a 25-horsepower steam engine to aid his biscuit-making processes. In 1851 Palmer introduced a revolving oven based on one that had been developed for ship's biscuits. It was 6 m long by 1.4 m wide (20 by 4½ ft) and enabled biscuits to be baked in a continuous flow. By this time Palmer had also succeeded in mechanizing dough-mixing processes with two different machines, one for hard-dough plain biscuits and one for softer dough containing 'fancy' ingredients such as milk, butter, eggs and various flavourings. The hard-dough machine could mix 125 kg (280 lb) of flour in fifteen minutes. For rolling and cutting there were also two types of machine: the Captain's Biscuit machine for harder dough and the Cracknel machine for softer dough. These two machines thus represented a formal break between the hard-tack of necessity and the fancy biscuit of luxury.

Advertising

As their output of biscuits grew, Huntley & Palmers pioneered early distribution networks, using commission agents to approach family grocers all over Britain. By 1850 the firm's biscuits were being sold in over seven hundred shops in four hundred towns and were exported all over the world in colourful tins that were often subsequently appropriated for other uses. Their richly illustrated biscuit catalogues offered to shop owners a tantalizing selection of their hundreds of biscuits.

Marketing materials from the second half of the nineteenth century suggest a strategy very much aimed at children.

Some say that the Victorians invented childhood, and Huntley & Palmers' marketing materials for biscuits support this theory. Early on, the company worked hard to associate eating biscuits with the innocence and simple pleasures of childhood. This link was so important that it was also remarked upon in the *Morning Star* article on biscuits:

> If you watch the operation of packing Johnny Smallboy's box as he leaves home for the first time, 'tis a thousand to one but Johnny's mother will slip in a tin box of biscuits, with the injunction to eat one every day between school hours, the good soul remembering that Johnny's heart is much influenced by Johnny's stomach, and the little box will serve as link between the mother and her child – will bridge over the gulf that divides the pleasant memories of Midsummer from the coming glories of mince pies and Christmas – and will annihilate the distance that lies between the school house and home. And as the child grows into a man he will look on the biscuit as a familiar friend, and remember with kindly emotion when first it solaced him in his days of mourning.[4]

Huntley & Palmers' marketing imbued the act of eating biscuits with a deeply personal aura. Manufactured biscuits were a commodity, but Huntley & Palmers worked to make biscuit-eating seem like a quiet antithesis to the industrialization of modern life. This association of biscuit-eating with childhood was quickly adopted in other newly industrialized countries. A particularly stunning campaign was created by the French company LU, or Lefèvre-Utile, the surnames of the husband-and-wife team who started the company in Nantes, in 1846. At first LU imported Huntley & Palmers biscuits, but it soon began making its own, most famously the

Advertising poster for LU Petit Beurre biscuits by celebrated French illustrator Étienne Maurice Firmin Bouisset (1859–1925). His *petit écolier*, or little schoolboy, became an icon of both French snack foods and French illustration.

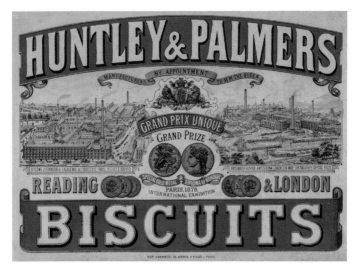

Huntley & Palmers poster celebrating their award-winning biscuits. Biscuit manufacturers were early proponents of branding grocery products.

Petit Beurre, which are extremely popular to this day. The campaign's pioneering poster, produced by artist and print-maker Étienne Maurice Firmin Bouisset in 1897 for a LU calendar, featured a wide-eyed schoolboy eating a biscuit and holding a basket bearing the letters 'LU'. The *petit écolier*, or little schoolboy, became an icon both of French modernity and childhood, and lives on today in an eponymous chocolate-coated version of the Petit Beurre featuring the image from the original poster. In France, a country that emphasizes meals rather than snacks, Petits Beurres came to corner the market as a simple, wholesome, not-too-sweet post-school snack and today have become as ubiquitous as a foodstuff can be in a country that prides itself on its distinctive regional gastronomic boundaries.

In Germany, food manufacturer Bahlsen, inspired by LU's success, introduced the Leibniz brand of butter biscuits in

The Petit Écolier, one of France's most popular biscuits.

1891. Leibniz-Keks were named after the seventeenth-century philosopher Gottfried Wilhelm Leibniz, a resident of Hanover, where Bahlsen was and is still based. 'Keks' was a corruption of the English word 'cakes', but the new biscuits became so popular that the term has become a generic label for similarly crunchy biscuits. One can find the Petit Beurre and the Leibniz, or its sibling the Choco Liebniz, in scores of countries around the world, so successful has their marketing been.

Packaging

Another way in which biscuits led the way in the global convenience food revolution was in their packaging. Here, a major U.S. company, Nabisco, was to be the global leader. In early America most baking was done by housewives. Commercial baking existed on such a small scale that any baking inventions were classified by the United States patent office as being part of the arts rather than industry.[5] Crackers, savoury biscuits that had evolved from hardtack baking, became popular throughout the country, however. These were not baked at home but were pioneered by such people as Josiah Bent, a retired Yankee ship's captain who started a bakery in 1801 in Milton, Massachusetts, after he retired from seagoing. Crackers were sold out of upright wooden barrels, and in nineteenth-century America the cracker barrel was an institution in the small grocery store. The freshest crackers were at the top, and the crackers became progressively more stale and grubby as the barrel's bottom approached. One story has it that when a customer complained about mice in the cracker barrel the store owner retorted, 'That's impossible. Mice could not possibly live in my cracker barrel. Because the cat sleeps there every night.'[6]

Another tipping point in biscuit and, particularly, cookie history occurred in the late nineteenth century when a prominent Midwestern lawyer called Adolphus W. Green saw possibilities in unifying American biscuit production and providing the consumer with a perennially fresh and appetizing product. Green united dozens of small bakeries that were producing a wide variety of products. The Uneeda Biscuit, a savoury cracker, was their first nationally recognized product; it was a phenomenal success, in part because of the promotional techniques the company used to sell these crackers.

Essential to the Uneeda's early success was the fact that it could be kept dry and fresh. Several experiments were conducted to find the right method to achieve this. George de

Choco Leibniz, an extremely popular German biscuit created in 1889 and named after philosopher and mathematician Gottfried Wilhelm Leibniz (1646–1716).

This Uneeda Biscuit advertisement was part of a campaign that paved the way for the mass popularization of cookies in the u.s. and worldwide.

Clercq, who had started his career as an office boy and risen to become a packaging expert at the National Biscuit Company (Nabisco), recorded the following early tests for the Uneeda Biscuit packaging:

> We took two pickle crocks and placed two porous bricks in each and put water at the bottom, but only enough so that the test packages could be placed on top of them without touching the water. In one jar we put sample packages in which we used a wax-impregnated paper; in the others, samples in which we used a wax-coated paper. We sealed the jars by putting paper tightly under the crockery lids. We left samples 72 hours. On examination we found the crackers with the wax-impregnated paper to be so soggy that they were unfit to eat. The others, enclosed in the package with the wax-coated paper, appeared to be unaffected by moisture and were in excellent, fresh condition.[7]

Tea Rusk and Brick House in New York City, oil painting on slate paper by American artist William P. Chappel, *c.* 1870s. Cookies and other baked items were often hawked by boys and young men in American cities.

With the input of other experts, Nabisco came up with its unique packaging: a sheet of waxed paper was placed over a piece of cardboard, and both were interfolded to form a sealed, airtight and waterproof box called the In-er-seal. Uneeda Biscuits, intact and dry and widely available, took the country by storm, slowly eradicating the cracker barrel and small-scale food commerce. A mere six years after it started, Nabisco's annual profits were more than $35 million. This did not go unnoticed by makers of other foodstuffs, who developed their own versions of the In-er-seal. Thanks to a single biscuit – a cousin of the ship's biscuit – the eating habits of a whole country, followed by those of the whole world, would change forever.

4
Crossing Continents: The Twentieth Century

Animal crackers and cocoa to drink,
That is the finest of suppers I think . . .
Christopher Morley (1890–1957)

By the twentieth century biscuits and cookies had achieved technical near-maturity. Improvements and innovations in production did occur, such as the creation of more sturdily adhesive sandwich cookies, and flavourings and packages became more sophisticated. Nonetheless, a bourbon cream from 1910, the year this chocolate sandwich biscuit was created, looked – and would have tasted – similar to a bourbon cream from 1999.

Such material continuities belie complex biscuit and cookie foodways, this last word a term born in the twentieth century to refer to 'the eating habits and culinary practices of a people, region, or historical period'.[1] The century started with telephones being a relative novelty and ended with Internet communication being the norm. While the history of biscuits and cookies does not follow such a dramatic trajectory, biscuit foodways do offer small windows on to aspects of twentieth-century history, including nationalism, globalism and the inexorable incursion of marketing into the personal sphere.

Political Biscuits

One cannot discuss twentieth-century biscuits and cookies without mentioning certain topical biscuits that are closely tied to political history. Anzac biscuits (or cookies) are a twentieth-century biscuit par excellence. An acronym for Australian and New Zealand Army Corps, Anzac biscuits were created to honour the Antipodeans who fought and suffered huge defeats in the Gallipoli campaign during the First World War. Their key ingredients are rolled oats, shredded coconut and golden syrup, and, though one can find them in several corners of the world, they are very much associated with Australia and New Zealand, where consuming them can be seen as an act of patriotism.

The Mexican wedding cake was perhaps the most political biscuit of the twentieth century. A buttery, rich, shortbread-type special occasion cookie covered in powdered sugar, it is identical in composition to the Russian tea cake. Several

Anzac biscuits are a tribute to First World War soldiers from Australia and New Zealand.

Mexican wedding cake has its origins in medieval Arabia.

historians have speculated that when relations between Russia and the U.S. became strained in the 1950s, a new, non contentious Central American cookie name was co-opted. If true, this biscuit provides concrete evidence of Cold War relations. This chapter in the Mexican wedding cake (or Russian tea cake, depending on your political persuasions) is but the latest in a history that stretches back centuries, to Arabia, via Moorish Spain, where similar cookies can still be found in bakeries across the Middle East, making the Mexican wedding cake a paragon of both semantic and geographical migrations.

A very old English biscuit, the Shrewsbury cake or biscuit, assumed a new identity under the British Raj, which ended in India in 1947. It is one of the oldest continuously made biscuits in England: records of a 'cake' made in the Shropshire town of Shrewsbury survive from the sixteenth century.

Indian biscuit seller. Biscuits, which have a long shelf-life, are convenient stock in shops across the world.

It contained lemon zest and sometimes dried fruit and was especially noted for its crispness, a characteristic remarked upon in a 1700 play by William Congreve in which a character uses the expression 'short as a Shrewsbury cake'. A shop in Shrewsbury made them to a secret recipe until the Second World War, when, like many other biscuits in the UK and Europe, production – and thus popularity – dipped due to the wartime rationing of such paramount ingredients as butter and sugar. Post-war, British supermarkets began to make their own-brand versions, many of which migrated unrecognizably from traditional recipes and were made in 'jam-sandwich' versions. A more authentic, traditional recipe is followed closely in Pune, in India's Maharashtra, where the Kayani Bakery is the most famous of a clutch of bakeries producing a wildly popular Shrewsbury biscuit that has come to be considered a 'local' speciality. The Kayani Bakery was founded in 1955 by Zoroastrians, many of whom were known to be Anglophiles during the Raj.

The Shrewsbury cake was one of several biscuits to qualify for inclusion in Euroterroirs, a European Union initiative to create a record of foods produced in a single locale for at least three generations. Many biscuits in the study went on to achieve official designations such as protected designation of origin (PDO) and protected geographical indication (PGI). They include several biscuits already mentioned in this book, such as *paximadia* from Crete, as well as Andalusian *polvorones de estepa*, a shortbread-type confection with nuts; *ricciarelli di Siena*, a lozenge-shaped variation on a macaroon that is baked on rice paper; Czech *Karlovarské oplatky*, or Carlsbad wafer, a delicate yet elaborately decorated wafer from the famous spa town; and Polish *andruty kaliskie*, a thin, wide wafer that was

Kokis, a deep-fried, crispy Sri Lankan food made from rice flour and coconut milk and thought to have its origins with Dutch colonialists.

Carlsbad wafers, from the famous Czech spa town Karlovy Vary, have been granted protected geographical indication (PGI) status by the European Union.

created in the 1950s in the town of Kalisz specifically to enjoy while strolling by the Prosna river on a Sunday afternoon. While many have argued that a political entity such as the European Union has no business intervening in local food production, where biscuits are concerned, this twentieth- and twenty-first-century preoccupation with foodways has led to the preservation and celebration of biscuits and cookies that might otherwise have become largely forgotten, if not extinct.

Marketing

Since the twentieth century, in some parts of the world, the residents of particular places have been so effective at marketing their local or regional biscuits that these have migrated beyond their borders and become ambassadors not just for their home towns but for their countries. Italy, expert at promoting the local, was also in the twentieth century extremely successful at marketing and exporting a sense of Italianness through its foodstuffs (as well as its fashion, design and cars).

Saronno, a commune in the northern Italian region of Lombardy, became famous for its particular brand of bittersweet macaroon made from ground apricot kernels rather than almonds. According to biscuit manufacturer Lazzaroni, who make the most famous version, the Saronno amaretto came about in 1718 when, in order to mark the visit to Saronno of the Cardinal of Milan, two lovers hastily concocted a batch of apricot kernel-based macaroons, wrapping them in pairs to symbolize their love. In the 1970s and '80s a sophisticated party trick in Lazzaroni's export markets involved making a funnel with the thin tissue used to cover the pairs of amaretti di Saronno and to then light the funnel,

Amaretti di Saronno, an impressive modern Italian marketing and export success story based on a very old biscuit.

causing it to fill with hot air and suddenly take off and rise towards the ceiling; the flames consume the paper and its ashes come floating down to the ground. Many a well-travelled household in Europe and America still has at least one of the bright red tins that Lazzaroni created to contain these delicious confections.

Another traditional Italian biscuit, *cantucci* or *biscotti*, which follows the age-old twice-cooked method, is made by baking a long, rough, sweetened 'loaf' filled with whole almonds, slicing the loaf on the diagonal, and baking the slices until

Scottish shortbread is made by the millions every year.

Fig Newtons, a top-selling American biscuit first created in 1891.

they become dry. Although a speciality of the Tuscan city of Prato, they are popular all over Italy and in the late twentieth century became fashionable in sophisticated restaurants around the world. Unlike amaretti, they are not associated with a particular producer and are in fact often 'homemade' by restaurants or delicatessens. They are frequently offered alongside sweet wine, especially Tuscan Vin Santo, in which to dip them, as an alternative to a more formal dessert.

Scotland, in inverse proportion to its size, has been possibly the most successful country in profiting from exporting a biscuit. Scottish shortbread, one of the very simplest biscuits to make – a basic mixture of butter, sugar and flour baked to 'shortness' – is the de rigueur souvenir for the some 15 million tourists who visit the country every year. Shortbread companies have proved very successful at creating appealing tins to hold their wares, often featuring tartan and bagpipe players, and creative at producing 'assortments' of different shapes, such as Scottie dogs or petticoat tails, which are thought to have originally been made to mimic the bell-hoop petticoats once worn under ladies' crinolines.

Manufacturers of Scottish shortbread, much of which is produced on a very large scale, have succeeded in creating an aura of wholesomeness around these biscuits, a quality that many global biscuit manufacturers throughout the twentieth century also aimed to emulate, often with a bit of gimmickry. If you grew up in 1950s America you could hardly avoid knowing about, or even singing about, Animal Crackers.

American child actress Shirley Temple immortalized the Animal Cracker biscuit in her 1935 film *Curly Top*.

Penguin biscuits were the subject of a memorable British advertising campaign in the 1970s.

Introduced by Nabisco in 1902, these hugely popular cookies were inspired by the Barnum & Bailey Circus (although some sources suggest that small animal-shaped biscuits were first imported from animal-loving England in the late nineteenth century). The animal biscuits inside are quite plain and dry, and the packaging – a box with a string that was originally meant to allow it to be hung on a Christmas tree – is a large part of the attraction. Animal Crackers were immortalized by child film star Shirley Temple in the film *Curly Top* (1935), when she sang a song called 'Animal Crackers in My Soup'; most Americans growing up at the time would have known this song by heart and passed it on to their own children in the 1950s. The Animal Cracker's popularity is also captured in a poem by Christopher Morley from about the same time, the first verse of which opens with the declaration: 'Animal crackers and cocoa to drink, / That is the finest of suppers I think'.

American Girl Scout Shirley Barton selling cookies to her compatriot General Graves Erskine in the u.s. in 1945.

In England in the 1970s the warm and fuzzy triumvirate of animals, children and biscuits was marketed particularly successfully with Penguin biscuits, chocolate-covered oblong biscuits covered in bright foil wrappers and not dissimilar in attraction to a chocolate bar. These benefited from television advertisements featuring adorable, anthropormorphized penguins interacting with children and the catchy strapline 'P-p-p-pick up a Penguin'. In the u.s., children themselves have proved to be a powerful force in marketing cookies, and not just a marketing demographic. American Girl Scouts typically sell 200 million boxes of different varieties of cookies a year to raise money for their units, the most popular consistently being Thin Mints, introduced in 1951.

A Twentieth-century Icon

All biscuits and cookies tell a story, or several, but if one had to be singled out as being of its era it would likely be the chocolate chip cookie, a food icon of the twentieth century. Rare among modern cookies and biscuits, the chocolate chip cookie has a distinct and human (as opposed to industrial) provenance. In 1930 Ruth Graves Wakefield, a dietician and lecturer on food, opened The Toll House, a popular roadside inn in Massachusetts that served homestyle cooking. In 1937 she published *Ruth Wakefield's Toll House Tried and True Recipes*, which contained a recipe for Toll House cookies that had, apparently, been the result of an accident.

Wakefield had wanted to make chocolate cookies by breaking a Nestlé chocolate bar into pieces, melting them and then mixing the melted chocolate into the cookie dough. She was disconcerted when the broken pieces only half melted and failed to become incorporated throughout the dough. Her customers loved these Toll House cookies, though, and so many followed her recipe that sales of Nestlé's yellow bar chocolate soared in New England. In response, Nestlé soon introduced their 'semi-sweet chocolate morsels', with Wakefield's recipe printed on the packages. These morsels, progenitors of chocolate chips, saved the cook the trouble of having to cut up a bar of chocolate and marked a tacit pact between the home baker and big business.

The mystique of the chocolate chip cookie survived the ever-quickening pace of twentieth-century life. American women had less time to bake, but products such as Pillsbury's Chocolate Chip Cookie Mix, introduced in 1953, and its Ice Box Cookies, refrigerated cookie dough, introduced in 1957, helped save time to devote to the ritual of American domesticity that was home baking. In 1977 the glamorous Debbi

A tin of Nestlé Toll House cookies, the original chocolate chip cookies, United States, 1970s.

Cookies accompanied by a glass of milk are a combination especially popular in the United States.

Fields defied her critics, who said a shop selling cookies would never work, and opened a store selling 'homemade' chocolate chip cookies in California, many of them baked in-store, where the smell evoked the home kitchen.

By the end of the twentieth century Mrs Fields had more than three hundred branches in the u.s. and abroad and had attracted several imitators. The cookie and its aura of being home baked became popular in Asia and even in countries such as France and England, despite the fact that they had thriving biscuit-baking heritages of their own. Industry responded to this demand as well, and one of the top-selling cookies in the u.s. in the late twentieth century was Chips Ahoy!, a chocolate chip cookie first introduced by Nabisco in 1963 and which was the subject of many elaborate marketing

Chips Ahoy! cookies have benefited from millions
of dollars in advertising spending in the u.s. and globally.

campaigns. In a century torn between the ease offered by an
increasingly industrialized lifestyle and a yearning for a simpler
and more traditional way of living and eating, the chocolate
chip cookie came to symbolize the multifarious nature of
modern foodways.

5
Myth and Metamorphosis: The Twenty-first Century and Beyond

We should also look forward to a time when advanced, satisfying and tasty biscuits are being routinely eaten by pioneering tea drinkers in space, or in colonies on the distant moons of the great gas giant planets.

Nicey and Wifey, *Nice Cup of Tea and a Sit Down* (2004)

In the third millennium, biscuits and cookies are a truly global phenomenon. In one form or another, in most corners of the world, they are available around the clock. Their versatility makes them adaptable to new culinary climes, and their small-ness means that they can be easily tweaked for different markets. Biscuits once firmly rooted in a given country, such as the chocolate chip cookie, have migrated beyond their ori-ginal borders, and some companies have become so effective at marketing their brands that certain biscuits and cookies are as familiar to children in Beijing as they are to children in Boston, Birmingham, Bangalore and Brisbane.

Complex in provenance, biscuits and cookies also play a complicated role in contemporary eating, occupying a broad spectrum in their manufacture, consumption and identity. At

Oatmeal biscuits with cranberries, a 'healthy' take on a simple biscuit and cookie recipe.

one extreme sit cheap, heavily industrialized biscuits, bought and eaten in a hurry for a quick, sweet energy fix. At the other extreme, biscuits and cookies are held up as badges of excellence in home baking, painstakingly made and decorated with high-quality ingredients, or else bought as a costly treat from an artisanal bakery. Although the twenty-first century and third millennium are young, a handful of broad trends in biscuit and cookie history can be identified so far: a mania for home baking and media about home baking; the elevation of biscuits and cookies into luxury items; and the rise of increasingly sophisticated marketing techniques to create new markets for existing biscuits and cookies.

Home Baking

Stimulated in part by the recession that began in 2008, home baking is making a global comeback, as people seek to save money and find delicious comfort in their own kitchens. There is a huge market in baking and decorating biscuits and cookies, with such books as *Bake Me I'm Yours* and *Cookie Magic: Biscuits and Cookies with Big Attitude* celebrating the virtues of home baking and decorating biscuits, and whole arsenals of equipment, including cookie cutters in shapes as diverse as human foetuses, 'ninjabread men' and machine guns.

The Great British Bake Off, a UK television show, attracts millions of viewers, who passionately follow the fates of the amateur contestants who compete to make the best biscuits, as well as cakes and other baked goods. In 2015 then British Prime Minister David Cameron publicly stated his addiction to the programme and his support for the eventual winner, Nadiya Hussain. In the U.S., the website of lifestyle guru Martha Stewart hosts online competitions for the most accomplished cookies by home bakers.

In a world that is so time-poor, it is astonishing that such labour-intensive cookies as, for example, the Lithuanian *grybukai*, or 'mushroom biscuits', are still widely being made at home. A dough containing molasses, milk and either lemon oil or extract is shaped into mushroom stems and caps. These are baked separately and then joined together with white icing, typically with the help of a large tray of rice in which the mushrooms can rest while being iced. The stems are coated in poppy seeds to evoke dirt and the caps are coated in a brown icing coloured and flavoured with cocoa powder.

Like grybukai, the labour-intensive Greek Christmas biscuit *melomakarona* can be found in artisanal bakeries, and yet many households believe that authenticity can best be achieved by taking matters into their own hands. While opinion varies about whether to include nuts, the common ingredients are olive oil, orange juice, honey and spices such as cinnamon and cloves. In a final step, after baking they are covered in a honey and sugar syrup, and for many Greeks the

Lithuanian 'mushroom biscuits', a labour-intensive biscuit made for special occasions.

Melomakarona are especially popular in Greece at Christmas.

knowledge that Christmas is imminent makes them well worth the effort of making at home.

In Scandinavia, authenticity is a factor in why the cookie known as *pepparkakor* in Sweden and *pipparkakku* in Finland is so often made at home. These delicate, spiced biscuits with a scalloped edge come in so many variations that one Finnish cookbook cites a hundred recipes for pipparkakku! The name refers to pepper, but this is misleading as *peppar*, in Old Swedish, was the name used to designate spices as a general category and not the specific spice itself. In Denmark there are as at least as many recipes for the biscuit known as *pebernødder* as there are cooks, and people can become quite proprietary about their version. Even the name is subjective – some insist on calling it *pebernødder*, which means peppernut, while others insist on calling it *brunbrød*, or brown breads. They are typically made very small and contain ground almonds or filberts and several spices, such as cardamom, cinnamon, cloves, allspice and nutmeg.

Homemade biscuits, whether eaten for pure pleasure at home or else submitted to competitions, are very often of such a high quality that they are indistinguishable from those made by professional bakers. Indeed, the line between the best homemade biscuits and the best professional biscuits has become blurred, in a way that might please La Varenne, who might justly take some credit for this development.

Macaron Madness

La Varenne might also be amused by one of the great biscuit and cookie metamorphoses of the late twentieth and early twenty-first centuries: that of the macaron, whose profile has soared since La Varenne wrote his recipe almost four centuries ago. The financial and 'lifestyle' excesses of the past twenty years have seen a parallel rise in the popularity (and some might say near-fetishizing) of the macaron as a luxury item. Although the recipe has remained little changed – being made from meringue and ground almonds, with a sweet filling – it has been adopted as the darling of contemporary pastry chefs such as the Parisian Pierre Hermé, who colours and scents them profusely, creating such flavours as olive oil and vanilla or licorice and violet. Perhaps because their lightness and softness makes them hard to replicate industrially, macarons are the perfect vessels for the skill and whimsy of a chef. According to Hermé,

> Macarons only weigh a few grams, but that's enough to leave your senses quivering with pleasure. Their thin, crisp shell, slightly rounded shape, tempting colours and tender interiors draw devotees to devour them with their eyes, and caress their smooth surface. Their

French macarons, made in a rainbow of colours and flavours, have become a globally popular luxury item.

flavours solicit the nose and, when one bites into that crisp shell, the ears tingle with pleasure and the palate is finally rewarded.[1]

The macaron counter-revolution has reached it apogee in the Ladurée empire, which has become famous across the world for its multicoloured, delicate macarons, sandwiched together with a light filling. Many of the patisserie's branches – which can be found across Europe, the Middle East and the Americas – double as tea rooms, evoking the grand *salons de thé* of early twentieth-century Paris, which offered to women an alternative to the cafés largely patronized by men. These *salons de thé* were not celebrated for their macarons, but David Holder, the business supremo behind Ladurée's recent expansion, has created a compelling and highly visual myth that somehow conflates the two and has diversified the company's range into beauty products such as 'Bonbon Bath Foam' and 'boudoir' candles.

Media and Marketing

Most biscuits and cookies do not have such powerful associations as the chocolate chip, nor can they command the high prices of a Ladurée macaron, and yet many have become iconic thanks to the marketing power of such manufacturers as Nabisco (owned by Mondelēz International). With the Oreo, Nabisco has cleverly created an aura around the biscuit that means its consumption is imbued with a sense of individuality.

The Oreo is a 'sandwich' cookie made from two hard, crisp chocolate discs, bearing the Oreo name and the Nabisco logo and filled with a thin layer of 'cream', or sugar icing. It has become the world's best-selling cookie: almost 500 billion have been made since it was created in 1912. Its manufacturers have kept up with the times: in the 1990s the lard traditionally used for the filling was replaced with partially hydrogenated vegetable oil, and in 2006 the trans fats were replaced with non-hydrogenated vegetable oil.

The ritual of eating Oreos has something of a cult following: opening the biscuit and scraping off the filling first is a popular plan of attack, although many alternatives can be found in a quick online search. This ritual has at least in part been created by Nabisco, which has printed instructions for eating the cookies on its boxes and has found endless ways to incorporate the Oreo into different facets of eating and leisure. Oreos have appeared in a McDonald's McFlurry, the fast-food chain's ice-cream dessert, and in 2011 they were promoted in

South America in tandem with the popular 3D computer-animated film *Rio*, with stickers in the cookie containers that could be collected to win various prizes, such as movie tickets and a trip to Rio de Janiero.

Versions of the Oreo filled with dulce de leche and a banana flavouring are made in Argentina, but it is in China that it has evolved the most. Here, the sugar content has been decreased, in line with Chinese taste preferences, and the package size has been reduced to make it more affordable. Oreo recruited three hundred student brand ambassadors from thirty Chinese universities, whose tasks included going around on bicycles with Oreo-like wheels; distributing samples to hundreds of thousands of people; and organizing basketball matches to introduce the notion of dunking Oreos in milk as a form of slam dunking. This was backed by television commercials showing Chinese children twisting open Oreos, eating the filling and then dunking the biscuits in milk. After the introduction of Oreo Wafer Sticks – chocolate-covered wafers filled with chocolate and vanilla cream, adapted to the Chinese palate – Oreos became the most popular brand of biscuit in China. The country became the largest market for Oreos outside the u.s., and with its China sales, Oreo's global annual revenues broke the $1 billion barrier.

Creation Myths

If big businesses work hard to create stories around their products, individuals also participate in mythologizing biscuits. In England the minor cult classic book *Nice Cup of Tea and a Sit Down*, written by a husband-and-wife team self-styled as 'Nicey and Wifey', is a contemporary paean to biscuits (and the British habit of dunking them in a cup of tea). The

Chinese Oreos: Nabisco tailors their Oreos' ingredients and marketing campaigns according to the tastes and culture of individual countries.

biscuits Nicey writes about, such as the custard cream, are mostly industrialized, many of them originating with Huntley & Palmers and other nineteenth-century British biscuit manufacturers. The custard cream is a sandwich made of two rectangular biscuits with an ornate, stylized swirl design; the 'custard' filling is actually a vanilla-flavoured fondant. In a poll in 2007, nine out of ten British people voted it their favourite biscuit. In Nicey's tribute, he writes that

> This biscuit, perhaps more than any other, has the ability to warp the fabric of space–time and transport us effortlessly back to days gone by . . . With its baroque detailing, the Custard Cream defies us to pin it down to any particular period of history. It is tempting to think that it was knocking around in the sixteenth century, its ornate swirls providing the muse for such great artists as Rubens or Caravaggio, as they nibbled on one over a late morning cuppa. It is equally at home in any decade of the twentieth century and now through into the twenty-first.[2]

While Nicey's tone is tongue-in-cheek, the sentiment is reverent. He is advocating for the biscuit (and cookie) as an organ of nostalgia. His fervour is tantamount to that of artisan bakers or proud home cooks who extol the virtues of pure ingredients and authentic recipes. Of course, the ingredients and processes in the custard cream are not the most wholesome, but Nicey's point is that the experience of eating the custard cream *is*. Nostalgia is highly personal, as are food preferences, but the pleasure taken in eating biscuits and cookies is universal.

Nicey, although unmistakably English, can be seen as a kind of biscuit and cookie oracle. He looks backwards as well as forwards, anticipating a globalized world in which biscuits and cookies will always play a part, and will always carry a story that is wholly true, partly true or, most likely, a mixture of the two. In this world view, there is room for every biscuit and cookie that has ever been, and every biscuit and cookie yet to come, of which there will no doubt be millions.

Fortune cookies, which originated in Japan, are given out at the end of the meal in many Chinese restaurants across America.

Viennese whirls, a popular British biscuit inspired by but unrelated to Austrian pastries.

Appendix:
A Biscuit Bucket List

Abernethy (Scotland) The Abernethy has a double provenance. Some consider that the biscuit originated in the Scottish town of Abernethy, once the royal seat of the Pict kingdom. Another version of the story ascribes them to a Dr Abernethy, an early nineteenth-century London surgeon who suggested to a baker near St Bartholomew's Hospital that the latter's captain's biscuits would be improved with the addition of sugar and caraway seed. The baker, a certain John Caldwell, agreed, and named the popular biscuit after Dr Abernethy. While originally the biscuit contained little butter, today's Abernethy biscuits contain more butter, so are less dry, and no longer contain the caraway flavouring. They are pricked on the top.

Afghan (New Zealand) The origins of the name might be lost, but that has not stopped this biscuit from being a national institution. It contains cornflakes, cocoa powder, butter, sugar and flour and is topped with chocolate icing and a walnut half.

alfajor (Argentina/South America) A large, thick sandwich cookie made from a shortbread-type dough and filled with caramel or dulce de leche, among other fillings. *Alfajores* are an extremely popular street food and snack, especially in Argentina. Descended from an Arab confection containing nuts, honey and spices, the *alfajor* made its way to Moorish Spain and evolved into its present form in the nineteenth century when Spanish colonials didn't have the original ingredients and had to adapt the recipe.

Ashbourne gingerbread (England) The Ashbourne is an example of a regional biscuit that has survived largely thanks to the production of a single local bakery or company. They have been made since at least the early nineteenth century in the town of Ashbourne in Derbyshire by the Spencer family of bakers. The popularity of Derbyshire as a tourist destination has also been a factor in its continued success – many biscuits that might have otherwise disappeared have survived because they have been packaged and presented as souvenirs. Ashbourne gingerbread contains no eggs and is quite pale compared to other gingerbread. Another distinctive feature is that it contains candied citrus peel.

avioliittopikkuleipä (Finland) The name means wedding rings. These are composed of simple butter cookies, often cut in a ring shape, sandwiched together with strawberry jam.

baci di dama (Italy) The name means lady's kisses, which echoes the shape. A local biscuit that has gone mainstream through successful marketing and an appealing, if gimmicky, shape. Originally from Italy's Piedmont region, they are now made commercially throughout the country.

baicoli (Italy/Venice) A sweet biscuit made in the twice-baked tradition, a long yeasted loaf is baked then allowed to rest for a couple of days. It is then sliced very thinly, and the slices are baked a second time. Unlike cantucci, also a survival of this ancient technique, baicoli contain butter. Baicoli are commonly packaged in decorated tins featuring Venetian dialect and are often dipped into sweet wine or hot chocolate.

biscottini al'anice (Italy) Aniseed biscuit made across Italy in many variations of ingredients and shapes – the common denominator is aniseed. In some versions an anise liqueur is used to intensify the aniseed flavour. In Sardinia they are drunk with white wine.

biskuitschöberlsuppe (Austria) A soup in which lozenge-shaped biscuits are served in a rich beef broth. The biscuits are made of butter, egg yolk, milk and flour and are flavoured with nutmeg.

brandy snap (UK) A thin, lacy, sticky biscuit made from butter, flour, sugar and golden syrup that is rolled around the handle of a wooden spoon while still warm to form a tube that is often filled with whipped cream: a simple treat that delivers a dollop of decadence. They are flavoured with lemon juice and nutmeg, and sometimes brandy, according the cook's preference. The brandy was originally a requirement but became optional as time went on.

canestrelli (Corsica, France) A crunchy, dry, mostly square-shaped biscuit made of flour, white wine and sugar. Variations include the addition of raisins, aniseed, nuts, chocolate chips or lemon and substitution of chestnut flour for wheat flour. They are popular in Provence.

digestive (UK) A hugely popular, versatile, wholesome biscuit both in the UK and in other parts of the world, the name comes from a former belief that they had antacid properties. They are round and contain whole wheat flour, which gives them a slightly rough, earthy quality. They are not overly sweet and contain some salt, and go well with cheese, notably cheddar. They are also hugely popular as chocolate digestives, in which incarnation the top is dipped in chocolate, either milk or dark.

drømmer I ørkenens sand (Norway) Also known as 'dream' biscuits, they are made from butter that has been browned (but not burnt), imparting an extra richness. They are flavoured with vanilla and dropped on to the cookie sheet rather than rolled.

Fig Newton (USA) First created by a fig-loving baker in Philadelphia in 1891, the recipe and machine used to make this fig-stuffed cookie were eventually taken over by a Massachusetts company and then by Nabisco. The name refers to the Massachusetts town of Newton. The Fig Newton is one of Nabisco's top sellers, and recent versions have been made with other fruit fillings, such as strawberry.

fortune cookie (USA) The fortune cookie is a crisp, plain, medium-sweet cookie that is folded twice to enclose a 'fortune', which can range from the cryptic to the inane: 'You are a person of another time' and 'Love truth, but pardon error' are examples. Mostly found in Chinese restaurants in the U.S., where they are typically offered after a meal, sometimes alongside freshly sliced oranges, they constitute a light dessert and a conversation piece in one. Fancy variations exist – they can be dipped in chocolate and can contain engagement announcements and even an engagement ring for a proposal with a difference.

funeral biscuit (England) An important part of funerals in Victorian England, biscuits wrapped with paper printed with death notices or with biblical quotations were used to announce a recent death or were given out at funerals as a sort of going away present to the attendees.

ginger nut/ginger snap (International) These are perhaps the most obvious modern heir to the medieval infatuation with spices. They come in many shapes and sizes but are commonly flavoured with powdered ginger and are typically hard and crunchy. Most versions truly do 'snap' when broken. They have been co-opted into the machinery of modern biscuit manufacture, and are very popular in many countries, including the USA and UK. In New Zealand, where they are known as gingernuts, they are such a popular part of daily life that a book of records in New Zealand bears the title *60 Million Gingernuts*, a reference to the number of gingernuts produced each year in that country.

graibi (Lebanon/Syria) Popular in Lebanon and Syria, these offer a divine textural contrast. On the outside they are crunchy, but inside they appear to dissolve on your tongue. This effect is produced by the large amount of clarified butter, which has a lower water content than butter.

Hanna-tädin kakut (Finland) Translated as 'Aunt Hannah's Cookies', these light-golden-coloured biscuits are made both commercially and in the home. They contain cream, which gives them an unusually light texture.

hasselnødssmakåger (Denmark) Made with toasted hazelnuts, which are then ground and impart a dark brown colour to the biscuits, the tops of these treats are decorated with the tines of a fork to make a criss-cross pattern.

Hobnob (UK) A recent biscuit even by industrialized biscuit standards, this was created by the McVitie's company in the 1980s and was an instant success. It is a round biscuit containing oats, which give it a slightly rustic quality that belies the fact that it is mass-produced.

Ischeler tortelette (Austria/Hungary) A legacy of the Austro-Hungarian Empire, these elaborate sandwich biscuits, made with ground almonds, are filled with apricot jam.

Jammie Dodger (UK) A sandwich biscuit made of two round, pale shortbread biscuits with a jam filling. The top biscuit is perforated with a small heart, so that the bright red jam can be seen through it, a beguiling contrast. A very popular biscuit that still retains an aura of novelty.

janhagel (Holland) These biscuits started out as humble bits of dough baked together, intended for poor clientele or rabble – *janhagel* was a term that meant rabble or multitude. *Hagel* literally means hail, and in the nineteenth century a baker 'improved' the recipe by adding a topping of almonds and sugar.

julpepparkakor (Sweden) A ginger nut served all year round but cut into myriad shapes at Christmas, including farm and domestic animals, children, grandmothers and grandfathers.

kniplingskager (Denmark) These Danish 'lace cookies' are made with rolled oats, which give them their mottled, 'lacy' look.

kourabiedes (Greece) Made either into a ball but more typically into a crescent shape, these are baked for special occasions and religious holidays. They contain chopped almonds and the dough is chilled before being shaped. They are rolled in icing sugar after they have been baked. Most commonly flavoured with vanilla, they can also be flavoured with rose water and even Metaxa brandy. Similar biscuits are found in countries influenced by Persia, such as Azerbaijan, and in a star-shaped version they are popular among both Ashkenazi and Sephardic Jews for breaking the fast at Yom Kippur.

krumkaker (Norway) A descendant of the wafer, the *krumkaker* has been made continuously since the sixteenth century using an iron that can typically produce two biscuits at a time, many of them highly decorated. Traditionally they were made over the fire, but now one can buy electric non-stick irons. After the hot biscuits are removed from the iron, they are wrapped around a special mould to produce a cone that is then filled with whipped cream and cloudberries or cloud-berry jam.

langue de chat (France) A delicate, thin, oblong biscuit containing cream and often used as an accompaniment to fruit or sorbet desserts. The name means 'cat's tongue'.

Lepeshki (Russia) *Lepeshki* gives its name to many baked goods, one of them being a distinctive almond sugar cookie made with sour cream.

lusikkaleivät (Finland) These 'teaspoon' cookies are made with browned butter and are shaped in teaspoons before being tapped out on to the cookie sheet. Once cooled, they are sandwiched with strawberry jam. They are a regional speciality of the western province of Pohjanmaa.

ma'amoul (Middle East) A stuffed biscuit consisting of a shortbread-like casing that encloses a filling of pistachios, almonds and dates. They are shaped in often highly decorative wooden moulds and are especially popular in Lebanon, where they feature in both Christian and Muslim religious holidays.

Maria (Spain) This is the most popular biscuit in Spain. Created in England in 1875 to commemorate the wedding of the Duke of Edinburgh and Maria of Austria, they are round biscuits bearing their name stamped on the top. They became popular after the Spanish Civil War.

Milano (USA) A trademarked cookie of the U.S. company Pepperidge Farm, founded in 1937 by Margaret Rudkin and named after her family farm in Connecticut. After a trip to Europe in the 1950s Rudkin became inspired by some the fancy biscuits she discovered there and wanted to bring them to a U.S. audience. The company had begun by making Naples biscuits, a version of the sponge biscuit, that were covered with chocolate on one side. However, these biscuits used to stick to each other, and so the company decided to create a sandwich version, with the chocolate in the middle.

nankhatai (India) A popular Indian biscuit traditionally made at home with a mixture of ghee, sugar, wheat flour, gram flour and semolina and scented with cardamom. More recently the gram flour and semolina have tended to be replaced with wheat flour. In houses without ovens, *nankhatai* were often 'baked' on the stovetop, on a tray between two plates, or else the dough was brought to a local bakery for baking. It is a popular biscuit at Diwali, the ancient Hindu festival of lights. It is a round macaroon-shaped biscuit and often features a *chironji* (a large seed that tastes a bit like almonds) in its centre. Its texture is short and crumbly, much like shortbread, but some purists resent this comparison, claiming *nankhatai* as a purely Indian confection.

oatmeal cookie (USA) A cookie that crossed over from health food to confection in the twentieth century, it none-theless retains an aura of wholesomeness, justified or not, depending on the quantity of the ingredients, such as butter and sugar. Quaker Oats have been the force behind this cookie, printing recipes on packets of their highly successful brand of oatmeal.

ohrapiparit (Finland) A soft biscuit made from barley flour, a product of very cold climates because of the grain's ability to ripen fast. Its low gluten content produces a soft effect in these biscuits.

pasticcini di mandorle (Sicily) A soft, chewy almond-based cookie that is often made with a glacé cherry or an almond on top. Some versions are reminiscent of marzipan.

peanut butter cookie (USA) A cookie that became popular in the 1930s, dovetailing with America's love of peanut butter. Along with chocolate chip and oatmeal cookies, they are a staple of the home-baked cookie repertoire.

pletzl (Eastern European/Jewish) A sponge dough is used to make these crisp, traditional biscuits, which can be either sweet, sometimes lemon-flavoured, or savoury, made with onion and poppy seeds. Traditionally they are leavened with eggs and contain no fat, and so conform to Jewish dietary laws.

polvorone (Spain/Mexico) A speciality of the Andalusia region of Spain, these contain lard and nuts or spices and are covered in icing sugar. They are individually wrapped in a tissue paper bordered with a fringe.

ragkåkor/Ruiskakut (Sweden/Finland) Made to emulate the large loaves of rye bread that are a staple in Sweden and Finland, these are small, simple butter cookies made with rye flour. Like the bread loaves, they have a hole in their centre.

ricciarelli (Italy/Siena) A speciality of Siena, in Tuscany, these lozenge-shaped biscuits are baked on rice paper. They contain almonds, sugar and egg whites and are crunchy on the outside and soft inside. They are an example of the way a traditional biscuit recipe – in this case the macaroon – can be adapted with local variations to become a very particular biscuit associated with a specific place.

rich tea (UK) A plain, round, unassuming biscuit marked with even rows of perforations. It is not too sweet, and almost ubiquitous as an accompaniment to coffee and tea at informal gatherings in the UK. In a country where biscuit preferences are strong, it can be relied upon to please most people most of the time.

rokkekager (Denmark) An elaborate drop biscuit containing a wide range of possible dried fruits, spices and nuts. Typically, several kinds of nuts and fruits are included.

sablé (France) The name means 'sandy' and refers to the texture of these biscuits, which do have a slight grittiness. This is countered by their rich flavour, as they are high in butter. They originated in nineteenth-century Normandy.

salatini (Italy) A word encompassing a wide range of savoury, often cracker-like biscuits served with aperitifs. They are often flavoured with a cheese or herbs or spices.

snickerdoodle (USA) A cookie laden with nuts and raisins and flavoured with nutmeg. It originated with the Pennsylvania Dutch community.

soetkoekies (South Africa) A chewy sugar and spice cookie that is a legacy of the Dutch settlers in South Africa. Some versions contain wine or sherry.

suspirus (Italy/Sardinia) In the Sardinian dialect, *suspirus* means 'sighs'. These ball-shaped biscuits are yet another regional variation on the almond, egg white and sugar theme. They are coated with an icing flavoured with lemon.

taai-taai (Holland) A chewy biscuit made at Christmas. They contain rye flour and either molasses, honey or syrup, but no fat, and are flavoured with aniseed. They were traditionally baked in carved moulds and can also depict biblical scenes. Production was industrialized in the late nineteenth century.

Wienerstänger (Denmark) These 'Vienna fingers', topped with strawberry jam, are flavoured with grated lemon rind, iced with powdered sugar and bound with lemon juice.

vanillekipferl (Austria) The butter-rich crescent-shaped biscuits are made especially at Christmas. Their crescent-moon shape is said – perhaps erroneously – to date from the 1683 victory over the Ottomans at the Battle of Vienna, the moon shape being based on the Turkish flag.

zaleti (Italy/Venice) The key ingredient here is polenta (cornmeal), which results in their yellow colour. They have a long, oblong shape and contain raisins, rum and milk. The name means 'the little yellow ones' in Venetian dialect.

Recipes

Recipes are divided into two sections, historical and contemporary.

Historical Biscuits

These recipes plunge you into the early days of biscuits, when the art and science of baking were far less precise than they are now. Along with Bonnefons' recipe for *biscuits du roy* (see pp. 38–9), they can be seen as a mini history course on baking biscuits. The lack of precise measurements and temperatures can seem off-putting, but this is part of the fun of suspending familiarity, and it also does far more than words or pictures can to give you a sense of baking before the introduction of labour-saving devices. Not only will you experience what it might have been like to tackle something relatively unknown, but the resulting biscuits (except perhaps for the macaroon and the Toll House cookie) will taste different and have a different mouthfeel from most biscuits you might have tasted before.

This first recipe is from Hugh Platt's *Delightes for Ladies* (London, 1602), a palm-sized volume that went through several reprints. I made this successfully by using shortbread for the shortcake, ready-ground almonds and the juice of one and a half lemons. After the first baking – when the biscuits were just firm – I sprayed them with edible gold and then returned them to a low oven, baking for about twenty minutes in total.

To make Iumbolls

Take halfe a pound of Almonds, being beaten to a paste, with shortcake being grated, and 2 ounces of carroway seeds, being beaten, and the juice of a Lemmon: and being brought into a paste, roule it into round strings: then caste it into knots, and so bake it in an oven: and when they are baked, ice them with Rose-water and Sugar, and the white of an egge being beaten together, then take a feather and gild them, then put them againe into the oven, and let them stand in a little while, and they will be iced clean over with a white ice: and so boxe them up, and you may keep them all the yeare.

The following is one of the easiest historical recipes I have followed. It is taken from Terence Scully's translation of La Varenne's *Le Pâtissier françois* (1653; Terence Scully, *La Varenne's Cookery: A Modern English Translation and Commentary*, Totnes, 2006, p. 459). La Varenne's recipe is notable for the precision of the instructions compared to earlier recipes. Again, I used ready-ground almonds.

Macaroon

Get some almonds, as is directed in the chapter on Marzi-pan, then you grind them and reduce them to a very smooth paste. For one pound of almonds (for instance), add in as much again of powdered sugar and four egg whites; mix those together, adding in a little rosewater, and beat them right away in the mortar to make the paste very smooth, though it has to be rather soft.

When the paste is ready, lay out chunks of it apart from one another on some white paper; those chunks should be somewhat long with the shape of a macaroon, and sprinkle them on top with some fine sugar. Then put them into the oven to dry out until they become quite firm to the touch on top. The heat of the oven should be gentle, as in the chapter on Marzipan, yet the hearth should be somewhat hot so as to swell the paste and make it puff up.

Macaroon should be in the oven a little longer than marzipan since it is thicker: macaroon can be left until it is thoroughly dry, or until the oven has cooled. Nevertheless, good Pastry Chefs do not leave their macaroon in the oven that long in case it browns: they take it out before it is wholly dried out, but then they keep it warm on top of the oven for twenty-four hours for it to dry out slowly without losing its whiteness.

Skipping ahead a few centuries, recipes have become almost clinically precise, although the American tendency of using volume rather than weight measurements causes many seasoned European bakers to raise their eyebrows. This, the recipe by Toll House Cookie inventor Ruth Wakefield that spawned the chocolate chip cookie (see p. 81), is notable for the use of unrefined sugar and the smallness of the cookies. Only a few decades after its publication in 1937, chocolate chip cookies would be at least three or four times larger than the ones in this recipe.

Toll House Chocolate Crunch Cookie

Cream 1 cup butter, add ¾ cup brown sugar, ¾ cup granulated sugar, and 2 eggs beaten whole. Dissolve 1 tsp soda in 1 tsp hot water, and mix alternately with 2¼ cups flour sifted with 1 tsp salt. Lastly add 1 cup chopped nuts and 2 bars (7-oz.) Nestlé's yellow label chocolate, semi-sweet,

which has been cut in pieces the size of a pea. Flavor with
1 tsp. vanilla and drop half teaspoons on a greased cookie
sheet. Bake 10 to 12 minutes in 375°F oven.
Makes 100 cookies

Contemporary Cookies

These have been chosen for their range of techniques and varied
origins.

Chinese Almond Cookies

Adapted from Greg Patent, *A Baker's Odyssey: Celebrating
Time-honoured Recipes from America's Rich Immigrant Heritage*
(Hoboken, NJ, 2007)

250 g (2½ cups) unbleached plain (all-purpose) flour
1½ tsp baking powder
¼ tsp salt
225 g (1 cup) lard
200 g (1 cup) granulated sugar
1 large egg
2 tsp pure almond extract
36 blanched whole almonds
1 large egg yolk, beaten with 1 tbsp water, for egg wash

Preheat the oven to 175°C (350°F). Line two large baking sheets
with greaseproof paper (cooking parchment) or silicone baking
pan liners.

Whisk together the flour, baking powder and salt in a bowl.

In another bowl, soften the lard with a wooden spoon. Add
the sugar and beat until creamy. Beat in the egg and almond extract.
Gradually stir in the dry ingredients to make a firm dough, and
knead briefly until the dough forms a ball. If the dough crumbles,
sprinkle in droplets of water and knead them in.

Divide the dough into 3 portions. On an unfloured surface, roll out each one into a 30-cm (12-in.) cylinder. Cut each log into 2.5-cm (1-in.) pieces. Roll the dough into balls and place them about 5 cm (2 in.) apart on the baking sheets. Flatten each ball into a 4-cm (1½-in.) circle and make a shallow depression in the centre with your thumb. Place an almond into each depression and press gently into the dough.

With a pastry brush, paint the tops of the cookies (not the sides) lightly with egg wash.

Bake one sheet at a time (leave the second sheet uncovered at room temperature) for about 15 minutes, until the cookies are a pale gold colour on top and the bottoms are a very light brown. Transfer the cookies to wire cooling racks to cool completely.
Makes 36 cookies

Basic Lebkuchen Dough (Germany)
Adapted from Sarah Kelly Iaia, *Festive Baking: Holiday Classics in the Swiss, German and Austrian Traditions* (New York, 1988)

350 g (3½ cups) plain (all-purpose) flour
1 tsp baking soda
1 tsp baking powder
1 tablespoon cinnamon
1 tsp ground cardamom
½ teaspoon ground cloves
½ tsp ground star anise
½ tsp nutmeg
½ tsp ginger
120 ml (½ cup) plus 2 tbsp honey
200 g (1 cup) caster (superfine) sugar
125 g (½ cup) unsalted butter
1 large egg, lightly beaten

Preheat oven to 175°C (350°F).

Sift the flour on to one sheet of wax paper and the other dry ingredients on to another.

Heat the honey, sugar and butter together over low heat, stirring all the time until the butter has melted and the sugar has dissolved. Do not allow the mixture to boil.

Remove the pan from the heat. Stir in the sifted spices. Gradually beat in the sifted flour, adding as much as is needed to make the dough, when stirred, pull away from the sides of the pan. You will need most of the amount given.

Allow the dough to cool for 5 minutes. If the pan is still very hot, remove the warm dough to the bowl. Beat in the lightly beaten egg and then knead the dough with your hands first in the pan or bowl, then briefly on a flat surface. If the dough is too sticky to handle, knead in a little more flour until it no longer sticks to your hands. If not using immediately, wrap the warm dough in plastic wrap and leave at room temperature until it is required.

Allow dough to rest overnight. Roll out to a ½-cm (¼-in.) thickness and cut out into simple geometric shapes such as stars, hearts or rectangles. Brush with beaten egg. Decorate corners or tips with split almonds, and a glacé/candied cherry in the centre.

Bake in the middle of the oven for about 15 minutes, or until lightly coloured and puffed. Loosen with a metal spatula and leave on the baking sheet for a couple of minutes to firm slightly. Finish cooling on wire racks. Can be stored in an airtight container for at least three months.

Makes 25 to 35 depending on size

Graibi (Lebanon)

Adapted from Greg Patent, *A Baker's Odyssey: Celebrating Time-honoured Recipes from America's Rich Immigrant Heritage* (Hoboken, NJ, 2007)

225 g (1 cup) clarified butter (or ghee)
125 g (1 cup) icing (confectioner's) sugar, plus additional for dusting
1 tsp rose water or orange flower water
¼ tsp salt
200 g (2 cups) unbleached plain (all-purpose) flour

Adjust an oven rack to centre position and preheat oven to 150°C (300°F). Line a baking sheet with parchment.

Put the clarified butter or ghee into a medium bowl. Use a wooden spoon to stir and soften it. Add the sugar and beat well until creamy and smooth. Beat in the rose water or orange flower water and salt. Gradually stir in the flour to make a firm, smooth, plaint dough.

To shape the cookies, scoop up a rounded tablespoonful of dough for each cookie, roll the dough between your palms to form a tapered cylinder about 9 cm (3½ in.) long and bend it to form a crescent. Place the cookies about 2.5 cm (1 in.) apart on the prepared sheet.

Bake the cookies for 20 to 25 minutes, until just cooked through. Do not allow the cookies to brown. Let the cookies cool on the baking sheet for 5 minutes, then transfer to wire cooling racks with a metal spatula. Careful – the cookies are fragile at this point. Let cool completely.

Dust the cookies with icing sugar before serving. Store the cookies in an airtight container at room temperature, layered between wax paper, for up to 2 weeks.

Makes 30 cookies

Melomakarona (Greece)

Adapted from Greg Patent, *A Baker's Odyssey: Celebrating Time-honoured Recipes from America's Rich Immigrant Heritage* (Hoboken, NJ, 2007)

For the dough:
225 g (2 cups) unbleached plain (all-purpose) flour, plus up to 150 g (1¼ cups) for kneading
2 tsp baking powder
¼ tsp salt
250 ml (1 cup) olive oil
75 g (⅓ cup) granulated sugar
finely grated zest of 1 orange
175 ml (¾ cup) freshly squeezed orange juice

75 ml (⅓ cup) cup brandy
175 g (1 cup) fine semolina
1½ tsp ground cinnamon
½ tsp ground allspice
¾ tsp ground cloves
100 g (¾ cup) walnuts

For the syrup:
175 ml (¾ cup) honey
150 g (¾ cup) granulated sugar
300 ml (1¼ cups) water
25 g (¼ cup) finely chopped walnuts

To make the dough, in a medium bowl whisk together the 225 g flour, baking powder and salt.

In a large bowl, whisk together the olive oil and sugar to combine well. Whisk in the orange zest, orange juice and brandy. Gradually add the flour mixture, whisking until smooth. Use a wooden spoon to stir in the semolina, spices and walnuts. The dough will be quite soft, oily and wet.

Flour your work surface with 60 g (½ cup) flour and scrape the dough on to it. Have ready another 60 g flour. Dust the top of the dough with some of the flour and knead the dough until the flour is completely absorbed. If the dough still feels sticky, gradually add some of the remaining flour, kneading it in until the dough feels smooth, soft and only slightly oily; it should not be sticky. It should feel rather like a soft bread dough. Depending on the humidity, you may need to use all the ½ cup flour plus another 30 g (¼ cup), possibly a bit more. If in doubt, err on the side of a bit less rather than more. Slip the dough into a resealable plastic bag or wrap it in plastic and let it rest at room temperature for about 30 minutes.

Adjust two oven racks to divide the oven into thirds and preheat the oven to 175°C (350°F). Line two baking sheets with silicone liners or baking parchment. Have a jelly-roll pan or small Swiss roll tin ready.

Turn the dough out on to your work surface. Pat it into a rectangle measuring roughly 13 by 23 cm (9 by 5 in.). Score the dough into 30 even pieces and cut them with a sharp knife. Roll each piece between your palms into an oval about 5 cm (2 in.) long and place them 5 cm apart on the lined sheets, 15 cookies to a sheet.

Bake for about 30 minutes, until the cookies are golden-brown, feel dry on top and spring back when pressed. Rotate the sheets top to bottom and back to front once during baking to ensure even browning.

While the cookies bake, prepare the syrup. Combine the honey, sugar and water in a medium heavy saucepan and bring to the boil over medium heat, stirring occasionally. Reduce heat to low and simmer for 10 minutes. Remove from the heat.

As soon as the cookies are done, transfer with a wide metal spatula to the jelly-roll pan, putting them close together with just a little space between them. Spoon the hot syrup evenly over the hot cookies. Let stand for 15 minutes. Carefully turn the cookies over and let them stand for another 15 minutes, or until the syrup is absorbed. Turn the cookies right side up and sprinkle them with the walnuts. If there is still some syrup left in the pan, transfer the cookies to another pan. Cover the cookies loosely with a sheet of wax paper and let them stand overnight at room temperature before eating. Store in an airtight container for up to two weeks.
Makes 30 cookies

References

Introduction

1 'Captain Scott Letter, 1911', www.huntleyandpalmers.org.uk, accessed 6 November 2018.
2 Alan Davidson, *The Oxford Companion to Food* (Oxford, 2014), p. 82.

1 Survival and Celebration: Fifth Century BC to 1485

1 For an understanding of biscuits in the ancient world and of paximadia in particular, I am most grateful for Andrew Dalby's excellent book *Food in the Ancient World from A to Z* (London, 2003).
2 Ibid.
3 Christopher Grocock and Sally Grainger, *Apicius* (Totnes, 2006), p. 253.
4 I am grateful to the superb scholarship of Janny de Moor for much of the research for the history of the wafer. See Janny de Moor, 'The Wafer and its Roots', in *Look and Feel, Oxford Symposium on Food and Cookery 1993*, ed. Harlan Walker (Totnes, 1994).
5 Constance B. Hieatt and Sharon Butler, eds, *Curye on Inglysch: English Culinary Manuscripts of the Fourteenth Century*

(including the 'Forme of Curye') (Oxford, 1985), pp. 2–3.

6 Eileen Power, *The Goodman of Paris (Le Ménagier de Paris): A Treatise on Moral and Domestic Economy by a Citizen of Paris, c. 1393* (London, 1992), p. 157.

7 I am indebted to the in-depth scholarship of Sarah Kelly Iaia for this section on German baking. See Sarah Kelly Iaia, *Festive Baking: Holiday Classics in the Swiss, German, and Austrian Traditions* (New York, 1988).

8 Malcolm Jones, *The Secret Middle Ages* (Stroud, 2002), pp. 1–12.

9 Charles Perry, *A Baghdad Cookery Book*, Petit Propos Culinaires 79 (Totnes, 2005), p. 102.

2 Sweetness and Lightness: 1485–1800

1 Sidney W. Mintz, *Sweetness and Power: The Place of Sugar in Modern History* (New York, 1985), p. 88.

2 Translation by the author, based on the translation by Barbara Ketcham Wheaton in *Savouring the Past: The French Kitchen and Table from 1300 to 1789* (London, 1983), p. 178. The original French recipe appears in Nicolas de Bonnefons, *Les Delices de la campagne* (Paris, 1679), pp. 18–19.

3 Philip Hyman and Mary Hyman, *Food: A Culinary History from Antiquity to the Present* (New York, 1999), p. 307.

4 Terence Scully, *La Varenne's Cookery: A Modern English Translation and Commentary* (Totnes, 2006), pp. 117–18.

5 Robert May, *The Accomplisht Cook, Or the Art and Mystery of Cookery* (London, 1685), p. 276.

6 François Massialot, *The Court and Country Cook*, trans. from the French by 'J.K.' (London, 1702), p. 93.

7 Rebecca Price, *The Compleat Cook, or Secrets of a Seventeenth-century Housewife*, compiled and introduced by Madeleine Masson (London, 1974), p. 256.

8 Peter Rose, *Matters of Taste: Dutch Recipes with an American Connection* (Albany, NY, 2002), p. 19.

9 Donna Barnes and Peter Rose, *Matters of Taste: Food and*

Drink in Seventeenth-century Dutch Art and Life (Albany, NY, 2002), pp. 36–7.

10 Gaitri Pagrach-Chandra, *Windmills in my Oven: A Book of Dutch Baking* (Totnes, 2002), p. 119.

11 Ibid.

12 Ibid., p. 111.

13 Rose, *Matters of Taste: Dutch Recipes*, p. 27.

14 Andrew Beahrs, 'Birth of an American Cookie', www.huffingtonpost.com, 30 November 2010, updated 25 May 2011.

3 The Golden Age: The Nineteenth Century

1 *Morning Star*, Wednesday, 26 September 1860.

2 T.A.B. Corley, 'Nutrition, Technology, and the Growth of the British Biscuit Industry, 1820–1900', in *The Making of the Modern British Diet*, ed. Derek J. Oddy and Derek S. Miller (London, 1976), p. 22.

3 I am indebted to the following book for background on Huntley & Palmers: T.A.B. Corley, *Quaker Enterprise in Biscuits: Huntley and Palmers of Reading, 1822–1972* (London, 1972).

4 *Morning Star*, Wednesday, 26 September 1860.

5 William Cahn, *Out of the Cracker Barrel: The Nabisco Story from Animal Crackers to Zu-zus* (New York, 1969), p. 27.

6 Ibid., p. 31.

7 Ibid., p. 73.

4 Crossing Continents: The Twentieth Century

1 www.merriam-webster.com/dictionary/foodways, accessed 25 October 2018.

5 Myth and Metamorphosis:
The Twenty-first Century and Beyond

1 Pierre Hermé, www.pierreherme.com.
2 'Nicey' and 'Wifey', *Nice Cup of Tea and a Sit Down*
  (London, 2007), pp. 84–6.

Bibliography

Barnes, Donna R., and Peter G. Rose, *Matter of Taste: Food and Drink in Seventeenth-century Dutch Art and Life* (Albany, NY, 2002)

Cahn, William, *Out of the Cracker Barrel: The Nabisco Story from Animal Crackers to Zu-zus* (New York, 1969)

Corley, T.A.B., 'Nutrition, Technology, and the Growth of the British Biscuit Industry, 1820–1900', in *The Making of the Modern British Diet*, ed. Derek J. Oddy and Derek S. Miller (London, 1976), pp. 13–25

—, *Quaker Enterprise in Biscuits: Huntley and Palmers of Reading, 1822–1972* (London, 1972)

Dalby, Andrew, *Food in the Ancient World from A to Z* (London, 2003)

Davidson, Alan, *The Oxford Companion to Food* (Oxford, 1999)

de Moor, Janny, 'The Wafer and its Roots', in *Look and Feel: Oxford Symposium on Food and Cookery 1993*, ed. Harlan Walker (Totnes, 1994), pp. 119–27

Grocock, Christopher, and Sally Grainger, *Apicius* (Totnes, 2006)

Hyman, Philip, and Mary Hyman, *Food: A Culinary History from Antiquity to the Present* (New York, 1999)

Iaia, Sarah Kelly, *Festive Baking: Holiday Classics in the Swiss, German, and Austrian Traditions* (New York, 1988)

Jones, Malcolm, *The Secret Middle Ages* (Stroud, 2002)

Mason, Laura, with Catherine Brown, *Traditional Foods of Britain: An Inventory* (Totnes, 2004)

Massialot, François, *The Court and Country Cook*, trans. from the French by 'J. K.' (London, 1702)

May, Robert, *The Accomplisht Cook, or The Art and Mystery of Cookery* (London, 1685)

Mintz, Sidney W., *Sweetness and Power: The Place of Sugar in Modern History* (New York, 1985)

'Nicey' and 'Wifey', *Nice Cup of Tea and a Sit Down* (London, 2007)

Pagrach-Chandra, Gaitri, *Windmills in my Oven: A Book of Dutch Baking* (Totnes, 2002)

Patent, Greg, *A Baker's Odyssey: Celebrating Time-honoured Recipes from America's Rich Immigrant Heritage* (Hoboken, NJ, 2007)

Perry, Charles, *A Baghdad Cookery Book*, Petit Propos Culinaires 79 (Totnes, 2005)

Power, Eileen, *The Goodman of Paris (Le Ménagier de Paris): A Treatise on Moral and Domestic Economy by a Citizen of Paris, c. 1393* (London, 1992)

Price, Rebecca, *The Compleat Cook, or Secrets of a Seventeenth-century Housewife*, compiled and introduced by Madeleine Masson (London, 1974)

Rose, Peter, *Matters of Taste: Dutch Recipes with an American Connection* (Albany, NY, 2002)

Scully, Terence, *La Varenne's Cookery: A Modern English Translation and Commentary* (Totnes, 2006)

Wheaton, Barbara Ketcham, *Savouring the Past: The French Kitchen and Table from 1300 to 1789* (London, 1983)

Websites and Associations

American Bakers Association Cookie and Cracker Academy
www.americanbakers.org/cca/

The Biscuit Doctor
www.thebiscuitdoctor.com

Biscuit People: The Global Biscuit Industry Overview
www.biscuitpeople.com

Biscuit Poetry
biscuitpoetry.blogspot.co.uk

Cookie Exchange
www.cookie-exchange.com

Girl Scout Cookies
www.girlscouts.org/en/cookies/all-about-cookies.html

Great British Chefs Biscuit Recipes
www.greatbritishchefs.com/collections/biscuit-recipes

The Huntley & Palmers Collection
www.huntleyandpalmers.org.uk

Joy of Baking
www.joyofbaking.com

Nice Cup of Tea and a Sit Down
www.nicecupofteaandasitdown.com

Acknowledgements

I would like to thank Michael Leaman, Rebecca Ratnayake, Amy Salter and Aimee Selby at Reaktion Books. I would also like to thank fellow food historians Ivan Day, Jane Levi, Laura Mason, Helen Saberi and Barbara Ketcham Wheaton, who at various times and in various ways provided encouragement, inspiration and helpful suggestions. I am grateful to Tommy Taborn-Letts, who was a brilliant and resourceful picture editor. Finally, I would especially like to thank Stefan Cucos for his constant support.

Photo Acknowledgements

The author and publishers wish to express their thanks to the below sources of illustrative material and/or permission to reproduce it. Some locations of artworks are also given below, in the interests of brevity:

Alleko/iStock images: p. 71; Antonio Gravante/Alamy Stock Photos: p. 32; billnoll/iStock images: p. 54; CTK/Alamy Stock Photos: p. 74; Chris Dorney/Shutterstock: p. 79; D. Pimborough/Shutterstock: p. 96; digitalreflections/Shutterstock.com: p. 82; Fabrizio Troiani/Alamy Stock Photos: p. 29; Gemäldegalerie, Berlin: p. 50; George W. Bailey/Shutterstock: pp. 65, 84; Highviews/Shutterstock: p. 47; igermz/iStock images: p. 20; The J. Paul Getty Museum: pp. 18, 40; Jiri Hera/Shutterstock.com: p. 95; Keith Homan/Shutterstock: p. 64; Library of Congress, Washington, DC: p. 22; Luigi Morbidelli/iStock images: p. 21; The Metropolitan Museum of Art, New York: pp. 9, 10, 16, 24, 25, 67; Milleflore-Images/iStock images: p. 70; Mitzy/Shutterstock: p. 59; Moskwa/Shutterstock: p. 28; Olexandr Panchenko/Shutterstock: p. 46; Only-Fabrizio/Shutterstock: p. 75; Paul Fearn/Alamy Stock Photos: p. 66; Pixabay (Wikimedia Commons): p. 91; private collection: p. 39; Pxhere (Wikimedia Commons): p. 83; Rijksmuseum, Amsterdam: p. 43; Science Museum, London/image Wellcome Trust: p. 13; Shootdiem/iStock images: p. 15; Siyapath/Shutterstock: p. 73; photo Stella/Shutterstock.com: p. 89; Steve Speller/Alamy Stock Photos: p. 72; Svetl/iStock images: p. 6; Tang Yang Song/

Index

italic numbers refer to illustrations; **bold** to recipes